BONSAI

A NOVEL

JUDITH BLEVINS
AND CARROLL MULTZ

BONSAI

Published by
ShahrazaD Publishing®
2189 W Canyon Court
Grand Junction, CO 81507-2574

Library of Congress Control Number: 2022900189

ISBN – 979-888525306-2

Contact the authors at:
judyblevins@bresnan.net
carrollmultz@charter.net

ALSO BY THE AUTHORS

Novels

By Judith Blevins

Double Jeopardy • *Swan Song*
Legacy • *Karma* • *Paragon*

By Carroll Multz

Justice Denied • *Deadly Deception* • *License to Convict*
The Devil's Scribe • *The Chameleon*
Shades of Innocence • *The Winning Ticket*

By Judith Blevins & Carroll Multz

Rogue Justice • *The Plagiarist* • *A Desperate Plea*
Spiderweb • *The Méjico Connection*
Eyewitness • *Lust for Revenge* • *Kamanda* • *Bloodline*
Pickpocket • *Ghost Writer* • *Guilt by Innuendo*
Gypsy Card Reader • *Waves of Vengeance*
Veil of Deceit • *The Journalist* • *We the Jury*
Star Chamber • *Reflection of a Killer*
The Gemini Connection

Childhood Legends Series®
By Judith Blevins & Carroll Multz

Operation Cat Tale • *One Frightful Day* • *Blue*
The Ghost of Bradbury Mansion • *White Out*
Flash of Red • *Back in Time* • *Treasure Seekers*
Summer Vacation-Part 1: Castaways-Part 2: Blast Off
A Trip to Remember —The R*U*1*2s Journey
to the Nation's Capital

Profile in Courage/Dedication

To **Edwin E. Multz** *and those like him,
who fought for the freedoms we
all enjoy, we are forever indebted.
By making Carroll's father our poster
child for a novel about World War II and
those who served in the Navy and Seabees,
we honor all the members of the military
and those who serve and protect
our nation in whatever capacity —
present, past, and future.*

*Insignificance can grow
into magnificence*

TABLE OF CONTENTS

A Note From The Authors

An olive branch in our culture has long been a symbol of peace. So has the bonsai—a tree or shrub in certain cultures that is a miniature of its larger counterpart. In addition to peace, the bonsai symbolizes harmony, balance, and order. Its symbolism, and the importance thereof, is not lost in the novel you are about to read.

At a time when survival of the fittest is in jeopardy, a symbiotic relationship between organisms must remain constant in order to ensure the survival of our species. Mutual interdependence requires coordination among all species in a recognition that the whole is only as good as its components. Disruption and lack of congruity are a recipe for extinction.

The mix of races, colors, and creeds is what made our nation the greatest nation on the planet. Taking the best and comingling it with the best is more than a genetic theory. It is a well-documented fact that a blend or an amalgamation of favorable traits spawns the superiority needed for an organism to succeed in a competitive environment.

In *Bonsai*, not only does nature produce the desire to return to one's beginnings or first love but the means to do so. By a twist of fate, a longing can result in an unimageable outcome. Never lose faith!

Our novel begins in the 1940s and spans the era between WWII and the Vietnam War. Not only did love of God and country bind Americans together through those dark years, but also the great music that emerged during that time that inspired us and gave us hope. The song lyrics are timeless and applicable even in today's world. Not only do our chapter titles serve as a clue as to what the chapter is about, but they're also a salute to the song writers who came up with such great music. Your authors hope the nostalgia will ignite fond memories.

Special thanks to Jan Weeks for her editing skills, Frank Addington for the cover and interior book designs; and Rosalie Stewart and John Lukon of KC Book Manufacturing for printing *Bonsai*, and finally to our readers, you will always be our inspiration.

Chapter One

Comin' In On a Wing and a Prayer

My name is Captain Steven Parker. I'm a United States Navy pilot attached to a carrier positioned with a fleet in the South China Sea. I fly one of the few remaining reconnaissance planes. After the attack on Pearl Harbor, the brass recognized the value of having a spy in the sky. However, when America entered the war, most of the recon planes were converted to combat planes and only a few recons were still in service. Because of the immediate high demand for trained pilots, having a copilot on any combat plane, much less a recon plane, would have been a luxury, so I fly my spy plane solo.

Today, typical of my past missions since the fleet arrived in the South China Sea, appears so far to be uneventful. My familiar comfort zone soon changes when the late afternoon sky suddenly turns dark and threatening. Thunder and lightning penetrate the cloud mass and high winds rock the plane. I fight with the control stick, trying to gain altitude hoping to rise above the storm. However, the plane seems to have developed a mind of its own and ignores my commands. *A lightning strike probably messed up my controls*, I think. I take a quick glance out of my side windows hoping to locate a familiar landmark. However, the rain is so heavy, I can barely see the tip of my wings, much less landmarks.

I don't have time to dwell on my predicament as my attention is directed to the obvious declining condition of the aircraft. When a sudden powerful gust of wind assaults the plane, the engines stutter and the plane lurches to the left. I say a prayer as I fight with the controls hoping my proximity to God's throne will be in my favor. Preparing for the worst, I steel myself for the inevitable crash. My guardian angel must be working overtime because I finally right the plane just before I come into contact with the massive jungle foliage. The overgrowth cushions the impact and I glide to a halt as I mow down the tops of stubborn and unyielding trees. I whisper, *Thank you, God*, just before my world goes black.

• • •

When I regain consciousness, with effort I force my eyes open. The sudden jolt of bright light stings and my eyes begin to water. I blink, trying to adjust to the glare, and instantly remember crashing into the jungle. Glancing around, I attempt to determine my surroundings as I struggle to sit up. To my surprise, I'm in what appears to be a hospital judging from the smell and looks of things.

"Ah, there you are!" remarks the man who is standing at the foot of my bed. Clad in a white lab coat with a stethoscope draped around his neck, he examines what appears to be a chart attached to a clipboard. Introducing himself, he says, "I'm Doctor Míng Jié." He then holds up three fingers, and asks, "How many fingers do you see?"

"Three," I respond, and then ask, "Where am I?"

His attention is directed back to the chart, and as he scribbles something, he explains, "You're in the hospital in Wai Sang. Your plane crashed in the jungle just outside our village, a few kilometers from Shanghai. The local coolies who work the rice paddies discovered you still strapped to the pilot seat yesterday after the storm subsided. You were unconscious, so they extracted you from the plane and brought you here.

"Considering the force of the crash, your injuries could've been a lot worse. You have a concussion, and your right leg is broken. Plus, you have a few bruises and scrapes, probably received at the time of impact."

I suddenly recall details. I remember I was on a mission when a storm knocked out my instruments.

Panic seizes me and I ask, "How long have I been here!"

"Since yesterday morning…" Then, after a brief pause and parodying with a Chinese accent, the doctor adds, "You lucky fellow, Captain Parker."

I sink back into the bed. Yes, I am *lucky fellow* I reflect remembering the trauma of the storm and how much worse things could've turned out. *My wing must be frantic wondering what happened to me. I've got to alert the fleet commander of my situation ASAP.* "Doctor, is there any way to contact the naval fleet currently located in the South China Sea…" I begin.

Dr. Míng Jié holds up a restraining hand. "Already taken care of," he remarks. "When you were brought in, I instantly recognized that you were a U.S. Navy pilot probably attached to the fleet. Using our ship-to-shore radio, I talked to your commander. When I explained to him the nature of your injuries, he asked me to tell you they would be working on an extraction plan to return you to the fleet as soon as possible. I let him know that the storm played havoc with the local dirt runways, and they're now muddy and unfit to land planes. The long and short of it is that it may be a while before they can send a plane to retrieve you. I assured him you were in good hands and that we would take good care of you."

"Thank you, doc," I say and experience a sense of relief knowing my commander has been alerted. It then occurs to me that the doctor has been speaking perfect English. "Where'd you learn to speak English so well?" I query.

"America," he replies. "I have a penchant for languages and speak several fluently. Because of my family's economic status, I was fortunate enough to be able to take advantage of studying abroad. That, of course, was before the war. After I had completed my preliminary medical courses in Beijing, I was accepted by Harvard where I earned a medical degree. Upon graduation, I did an internship at Walter Reed Medical Center in Maryland. During that period, the demand for doctors was great and I ended up staying in the United States for six more years.

"I was close to my parents and stayed in constant touch with them. When I learned my father had been diagnosed with inoperable lung cancer, I returned to Shanghai. After my father died, my mother was devastated. I was their only child, and she begged me to stay in Shanghai. As much as I loved living in the United States, I loved my mother more, so I stayed.

"My mother employed domestic help from the village of Wai Sang. It was through the peasants

I found out about this hospital and how desperate they were for doctors. I applied and was accepted with open arms. My time here has been fulfilling and I've never regretted my decision. The pay isn't so great, but the satisfaction I get from working with the poor more than makes up for it.

"I'm honored to have had the opportunity to live and study in America. It was an unbelievable experience which I'll never forget." Hanging the chart on the rail at the foot of my bed and securing the pen in his breast pocket, the doctor adds, "Before, when I said, *you lucky fellow*, I meant in more ways than one."

• • •

After the doctor leaves, I ponder his statements. *Yes, we Americans are very fortunate to live in a democratic society.* With that thought lingering in my mind, I fall into a fitful sleep. No dreams, only nightmares filled with fear, apprehension, and anxiety.

• • •

I stir when I feel a tap on the shoulder and hear someone say, "Time for pill."

I'm startled and blink sleep from my eyes. Everything hurts and I groan. My body feels like I just played a football game—and was on the losing side. I gradually regain my senses and find myself staring into the eyes of what appears to be a nurse. She's holding a small plastic cup. "I hope you're not waking me up to take a sleeping pill?" I mutter and try to ignore the pain as I struggle to a sitting position.

"You funny guy!" she says as she dumps two pills into my outstretched hand. "One for infection, other for pain," she explains as she hands me a glass of water. I get the message and obediently swallow the pills.

"That not so bad," she remarks more as a question than a statement and appears to be waiting for my affirmation.

"Not bad," I say to appease her. Apparently satisfied we're in agreement, she straightens my bedding. It's hard to guess the age of Orientals, but she looks to be in her late teens, early twenties. Her hair shines like black silk and is pulled back into a clip away from her face. Her tawny skin is flawless, and her face is highlighted by sparkling brown eyes and petal pink lips. The name tag pinned to her uniform identifies her as Su Lin. "Did Buddha send an angel to nurse me back to health?" I ask and grin at her.

"Oh, no! Not Buddha—Doctor Míng Jié send me," she says and smiles.

I can't tell if she's serious or not, so I change

the subject so as not to appear to be disrespectful to Buddha. "I'm starved!" I blurt, and she jumps back at my sudden outburst. The look on her face is priceless and I laugh. "Sorry, Su Lin." In a softer voice I ask, "What's for lunch or is it dinner time?"

"Yes, dinner. Today, chow mein. You *rike*?" Su Lin quires as she refills my water glass.

"Real Chinese chow mein! You bettcha I *rike*," I enthusiastically reply using my best Chinese accent.

Su Lin frowns and furrows her brow. "I go get dinner," she says and departs.

Was it something I said?

• • •

Hunger replaces anxiety, and as I wait for dinner to arrive, the patient in the bed next to me engages me in conversation. Mindful of my broken leg, I slowly turn to face him. The pain pill must be working, as I don't hurt quite as much as I did when I awakened.

"My name's Hank Mitchell," the patient begins. When he tries to reach over to shake hands, he immediately aborts the gesture. Groaning, he mutters, "Not such a good idea—busted ribs."

I nod and am relieved I don't have to stretch to shake his hand. Despite the pain medication, I still ache from head to toe. To aggravate it is not something I want to do!

"I couldn't help overhearing your conversation with Su Lin," Hank remarks. "And since you, too, are American and obviously not acquainted with Chinese customs, I feel obligated to warn you that it's an insult to imitate the Chinese because they can't pronounce certain English words."

Feeling like a fool for having unwittingly insulted her, I think, *So that explains Su Lin's sour expression and sudden departure.* "Thank you for the heads-up," I respond. "You're right, I didn't know and will be more careful in the future."

"It's taken me awhile. I've been in China for three years and am still learning the customs, so don't feel bad."

"Three years! What brought you to China?"

"I'm in the construction business." Hank winces as he readjusts his position by awkwardly propping pillows behind him. "My company has a contract to erect a hotel in downtown Shanghai. Last week, I slipped on some debris, and when I fell, I busted a couple of ribs and got this nasty gash on my forehead. After wrapping my ribcage, the doctors decided to keep me a few days for observation because of the concussion. With a little luck, I could be released as early as tomorrow." Hank winces as he changes position.

"With Hitler ravaging Europe, and now the Japanese attack on Pearl, Americans working in foreign countries are at risk and we may have to abort our project and return to the states to help with the war effort," Hank says. Pausing, he takes a swig of water before continuing. "Anyway, I've been thinking about joining the Seabees and the attack on Pearl was just the nudge I needed to take the plunge. I love construction and my experience could come in handy. Also, I'm a certified marksman."

"Right you are. And now, fighting wars on two fronts, I think our country is going to need all the manpower it can muster," I say. "I'm assigned to a carrier with the fleet positioned in the South China Sea. I crashed in the jungle late yesterday when my instruments were knocked out by the storm—"

"I heard about that!" Hank interrupts. "Scuttlebutt is you're one lucky hombre."

I make the sign of the cross. "My guardian angel must've been working overtime."

"Something was working for you. What's that time-honored adage? Fortune favors the brave! I'm told your plane was a total wreck and for you to have escaped with minimal injuries, well… that's a miracle in and of itself."

I never grasped the seriousness of the situation until my discussion with Hank. Having skirted death, I need to thank God for my survival. "I guess a broken leg and a concussion aren't so bad after all," I say.

Our conversation is interrupted when an orderly wheels in a cart laden with two trays of chow mein and other food items. As he serves me my tray, I'm disappointed it's not Su Lin. I look past him and ask, "Where's Su Lin?"

"She go home. I Hóng," he answers. He then serves Hank his tray. He then leaves.

I didn't realize how hungry I was until I begin eating. As Hank and I gobble down our dinner, hunger trumps manners and we talk with our mouths full.

"Another word to the wise," Hank says between bites. "Our volunteer, Su Lin, is hands off."

"Volunteer?" I blurt. "I thought she was a nurse."

"That's a common mistake since their uniforms are similar," Hank comments. "And I couldn't help notice you've taken a liking to her."

Embarrassed, I respond, "Didn't realize my interest was so obvious."

"You're a red-blooded American boy, aren't you?" Hank asks. "You'd have to be deaf, dumb, and blind not to appreciate Su Lin's attributes," he adds with a wide grin.

"Well, since you put it that way…," I begin.

"Anyway, how is it she's hand's off—married?"

"Naw! Nothing like that. I've been told her father is the mayor of Wai Sang. There are very specific laws and customs dictating conduct in the presence of unmarried females here in China. I was told high-ranking Chinese officials are especially particular about their daughters fraternizing with foreigners—especially Americans. The oldtimers still stick to the ancient form of punishment for disobedience. Old traditions are hard to discard... especially if they work," Hank says as he crams another load of chow mein into his mouth.

My curiosity is now piqued. "Okay, I'll bite. What's the punishment?"

"Death. At least for the disobedient female," Hank replies.

I gulp. "Are you kidding?"

"Nope, anyway I'm not sayin' it's true 'cause I don't know that for a fact. Just passin' on the skinny as it was handed down to me when I first got here."

We finish our dinner in silence. I'm stunned to learn that some ancient barbaric customs are still being practiced in certain parts of the world. Before going to sleep that night, I ponder the reasoning behind advanced cultures continuing the antiquated forms of punishment for disobedient females. It appears the female of the species are still expendable in many cultures and some things will never change so long as the methods work to control the masses. What about the offending male?

• • •

Hank is scheduled to be discharged the following morning and is up early chomping at the bit for his release.

"My foster father and two brothers fought in World War I," Hank says as he pulls on his socks. "One of his brothers didn't come home. I remember cringing when, usually over Sunday dinner, my foster father and his surviving brother exchanged war stories. I later realized commiserating was their method of dealing with the unimaginable things they were exposed to during the war.

"My foster mother would usher us kids into the kitchen to isolate us from hearing their horror stories. The inhumanity was mindboggling and still Germany persists in its quest to dominate the world—using even more cruel, violent, and treacherous means." Hank pauses as he slips into his work boots, and at the same time glances at me with determination in his eyes. "The next time I see a poster with Uncle Sam pointing his finger above the *I Want You* slogan, I'm taking it personally and answering the call."

"Hank, you're an inspiration and the kind of

patriot our country needs more of. Good luck and Godspeed."

Hank stands and looks around no doubt ensuring he hasn't forgotten anything. I'm sitting on the side of my bed as Hank approaches and extends his right hand. Ignoring the pain, our handshake turns into a bear hug. "Ouch! Ribs still tender," Hank exclaims and pulls back. He looks toward the door then back at me. "Don't know if you're a religious man, but my foster mother was a dyed-in-the-wool Baptist and made sure us kids knew the Bible, chapter and verse. She never preached hell's fire and damnation, it was always God's love and mercy. You'll be in my prayers, my friend. Take care of yourself!"

I'm moved to tears as I watch Hank exit our hospital room. *There goes a rare breed! He's a true patriot and inspiration! With faith and dedication like his, how can we lose?* My thoughts then turn to Su Lin.

Chapter Two

Fools Rush In

My prayers must have been answered, I say to myself as Su Lin appears in the doorway pushing a wheelchair. "Want ride?" she asks with a broad smile. Then apparently noticing my tears, she exclaims, "Oh, no. You hurt? I get pill," and she turns back toward the corridor.

"Wait! Come back," I protest. "I'm not in pain…"

"But you cry…" she remarks as she reenters my room.

"Not pain tears," I mumble. She apparently understands the implication and doesn't press for details.

After a few moments of silence, Su Lin says "Nice day. I take you to garden?" and raises her brow.

I don't know where the *garden* is, or even that there is one, but I reason anything would be better than this drab hospital room, especially since Hank has left. "I'd be delighted," I quickly respond, and with the use of crutches, I hobble to the wheelchair.

After I'm seated, Su Lin takes the crutches

and leans them against the wall next to my bed. She then spreads a light throw over my lap and turns the wheelchair toward the doorway. Much to my chagrin, we collide with the doorframe a couple of times before clearing the room. Luckily, the collisions occur on the left side of the chair. My right leg is sticking straight out encased in a plaster cast.

"You learn to drive in New York City?" I jokingly inquire.

My attempt at humor apparently goes over her head. "No. Hóng teach me," she responds. "I do good, yes? No hit injured leg!"

Su Lin's sweet innocence overwhelms me, and I have a sudden urge to cradle her in my arms and protect her from the evil raging across the globe. However, the moment passes when I begin to fear for my own life as we traverse the hospital corridors at a pretty good clip. I have a white-knuckle grip on the arms of the wheelchair, expecting to overturn anytime as we careen around corners.

After a few anxious moments, and much to my relief, we're suddenly outside and she slows the pace. The storm clouds have dissipated, and the warm sun feels good on my face. This is the first time I've seen the exterior of the hospital, and it takes my eyes a moment to adjust to the brightness.

As I study my surroundings, I notice the hospital's Chinese pagoda-style architecture, which seems out of character for a hospital.

Apparently noticing the expression on my face, Su Lin explains. "Hospital was temple long, long ago. No longer use, so village make hospital."

"Wise decision," I comment as I admire the multi-tiered pagoda towers. I count them. There are five stories. Each story has multiple pagoda-style eaves surrounding it. I'm obviously captivated by the architecture and preoccupied by my newly discovered environment.

Su Lin follows my gaze and must've picked up on my interest. "You *rike*?" she asks.

"Yes, I'm intrigued by your culture and unique architecture."

She nods and proceeds to maneuver the wheelchair. "I show you more," she comments. We circle the hospital and when we arrive at the rear of the building, we're in a lush garden. I notice how the grounds are meticulously maintained. With the pagoda towers in the background, the whole layout could be the cover of a Chinese version of *Better Homes and Gardens*. Su Lin slowly pushes me down a winding walkway and the pride in her voice is unmistakable as she gives me her best tour guide spiel. We pass water fountains, images of Buddha and other icons I don't recognize as we slowly traverse the walkway.

"So sorry, my English not too fine," she comments.

"The picture is worth a thousand words," I say. "Even without the commentary, which by the way is flawless, I have forever chiseled in my mind images that can never be erased."

"What all that mean?" Su Lin asks.

"Let's just say, I understand everything you said and couldn't have had a more perfect tour guide." Su Lin graces me with a wide smile.

We roll past vegetation with appealing names such as Manchurian apricot, flowering almond, bamboo, maidenhair, and fragrant lily. Upon reaching the end of the walkway, we approach an area that resembles a cul-de-sac.

"This my best place," Su Lin states and moves my wheelchair further into the cul-de-sac next to a small bench where she sits, keeping one hand on the armrest of the wheelchair.

"It's intriguing," I remark as I study the landscape. I count seven pedestals arranged in a semicircle around the cul-de-sac. Positioned at the top of each pedestal is a small ceramic-like pot containing a plant that resembles a miniature version of a full-grown tree. "What are those plants called?" I ask.

"Bonsai trees," Su Lin says smiling at me. "All very old."

To me *old* designates the twenty-year old peach trees in Gramps' orchard back in Georgia. Needless to say, I'm surprised, maybe even stunned, when she comments, "Bonsai can live many hundred, even thousand years. All these," she says and points to the seven trees, "over hundred years, maybe more."

She must be putting me on. How can a tree live in a small container for a hundred years, much less a thousand? "I'm speechless," I manage to utter.

"Ancient Chinese teach nurture and care, so trees live long time. I call place Bonsai Garden. No bad here, only peace and joy. I come often."

As we linger admiring the bonsai, I watch a bird with pink and gray feathers fly into the garden. The bird swoops down and lands on one of the miniature trees. Su Lin exclaims, "Look! Rose finch come. That sign good luck." In her enthusiasm, she reaches over and takes my hand.

Her hand is warm and smooth and fits perfectly in mine. Once again that urge stirs in me. However, this time it isn't parental, it's more than that. Even remembering Hank's warning about hand's off, I can't ignore what's happening and I think I'm falling in love for the first time in my twenty-eight years on this planet. *Is she feeling the same way?*

• • •

When we return to my hospital room, and after helping me into bed, Su Lin states, "I go see to lunch. You rest."

"Thank you, Su Lin, for the walk in the garden." I'm reluctant to let her go so I ask, "Can you stay and share my lunch?"

"Ah, no can stay. Hospital not allow. But… see you tomorrow."

"I'll be here," I respond. Su Lin then tucks the blanket in around me. When she leans close, I smell the fragrance of her hair and want to pull her to me but resist the urge.

After Su Lin leaves, I reflect on the walk in the garden and marvel at the revelation that the bonsai can live so long. Still pondering the mindboggling reality of the lifespan of the miniature trees, I'm jarred back to reality when Dr. Míng Jié gently raps on my open door. "May I come in?" he asks.

"Of course! Since when do doctors need permission to enter a patient's room?"

"Unlike Americans, Chinese respect privacy," he explains.

Don't know if that remark was meant to be an insult so I ignore the comparison of cultures and say, "Well, come on in anytime. You have my permission."

"Thank you," he replies and pulls a chair up next to my bed. "How are you feeling?"

"Much better," I reply. "Su Lin took me for a walk in the garden. I'm still reeling after being told how long the bonsai can live."

"Ah, yes. I, too, marvel at the ancient Chinese process that prolongs the life of the trees. Now, if we could figure out how to do that in humans…" Dr. Míng Jié reflects. After a pause, he continues, "Spoke to your commander this morning. I'm afraid I have bad news."

Oh, no! Now what? And I brace myself for the worst—whatever that may be.

Dr. Míng Jié pulls a chair close to my bedside. "It appears your fleet is carrying only jet fighters, no larger planes," he begins. "And because of the extent of your injury and having your leg in a cast, it would be impossible for you to fit into one of the jet seats—either front or rear. Therefore, you will have to remain here until we can take the cast off your leg."

"And that's bad news!" I blurt.

"Yes. Were you expecting something else?"

"No. In today's world you never know. Bad news can come in many forms. And I don't consider remaining here to be bad news. In fact, I like it here," I remark.

"Wonderful! We like having you but wish it were under different circumstances. You realize the cast must be left on for at least six more weeks?"

"Didn't know it was for that long," I reply. Then, thinking that will give me time to get better acquainted with Su Lin, I add, "You're the doctor! I do as you say!"

Chapter Three

Sentimental Journey

Since it's spring, the "rolls" in the bonsai garden have become a daily routine. Every day, the first thing I think of is my walk with Su Lin. Just being near her rejuvenates me. We've shared much of our history during her visits the past six weeks and have grown very close. I think back to those earlier visits.

Su Lin has two younger sisters and an older brother. Her mother, Hǎi Yún, was given in marriage at a very young age. The tradition back then was that families arranged marriages—not the bride or groom to be. Unlike Americans, the father of the bride is given a dowry by the groom's family. The larger the dowry, the better the bride!

Su Lin revealed that she suspected her mother was never happy and after the last child was born, her mother sank into a deep depression. The depression drove her mother to suicide. Her father, Wěi Qí, went off the deep end after her death and refused to be consoled. He dealt with his loss by drinking heavily for years.

During her father's alcoholic spree, the

children were supervised by a nanny who was a strict disciplinarian. When her father finally worked through his sorrow and sobered up, he attempted to make amends for lost time. He had always been critical of the local government, and having nothing to lose, he ran for mayor promising to make a difference for the citizens of Wai Sang. He was elected and succeeded in cleaning up the corruption and has been a favorite ever since.

By the time their father quit drinking, the children were old enough to take care of themselves and begged him to get rid of the nanny who made their lives so miserable. Her father agreed but warned them that he subscribed to family traditions handed down over generations. He would not tolerate disobedience or disgrace and that the children better live honorably—nanny or no nanny.

As I listened, it occurred to me that compared to her, my life was uninteresting and uneventful—even boring. When it was my turn, I kept my story light.

"I've two older brothers and we had a normal childhood growing up in rural Georgia. When I started high school, it was obvious those who were good at sports were the heroes to their peers, so I went out for football. Football is a rough sport and after a few months I figured out that being battered, bruised, kicked, and knocked down all the time wasn't my cup of tea."

"Cup of tea?" Su Lin looked puzzled.

"That's American slang for something you like," I explained. "I disliked skinned chins, bloody noses, bruised ribs, and broken bones, so I changed my interest to basketball, a much gentler sport."

"I see," she said and smiled. "Good choice."

"Hmm, I donno. I wasn't very good at basketball either. I was a lanky, awkward kid and didn't have much coordination. I was always tripping over my feet. My academic skills were far better than my athletic skills. However, I liked the competition, so I kept playing.

"Being part of the team and wearing the uniform in the school colors was cool. My one and only claim to fame happened during my senior year. I was thrust into the limelight when our team won the state basketball finals in the last four seconds of the game."

"What mean *limelight*?" Su Lin had asked.

"It's a term for being the star or a hero. I accidentally became a hero. You see, I had possession of the ball, and the clock was ticking off the last seconds of play. The arena was wild with spectators stomping their feet and cheering for their respective teams. It was a miracle that I even heard one of my teammates shout, 'Shoot! Shoot!' I made an overhead throw as a last-ditch effort."

Then realizing Su Lin probably didn't understand the term *last-ditch*, I reworded it. "That is, I made a desperation shot from midcourt by flinging the ball high into the air in the direction of the basketball hoop." Su Lin looked perplexed, so even from my wheelchair, I demonstrated the arm movements of an overhead shot. "It was an accident that the ball swished through the net and scored the winning points. My teammates hoisted me onto their shoulders and carried me around the gymnasium like a hero."

Su Lin gazed into my eyes as she begged, "Tell me more!"

Hoping to make her smile, I confessed that I wasn't much on the dance floor either. I told her about the time my senior prom date wore a gown with a long sweeping skirt. "I repeatedly stepped on the hem of the dress as we danced which created tension between my date and me not to mention the damage to the dress. Needless to say, that relationship died on the vine, and we never dated again. In fact, she never even spoke to me again."

Su Lin giggled, as I finished my story. "The rest is history," I said. "When I graduated from high school, I enlisted in the Navy, where I learned to fly and loved it. Flying is in my blood and after my first four-year commitment, I reenlisted. America entered the war shortly thereafter and I was assigned to the carrier fleet where I am today. And I'm grateful. Otherwise… I'd never have met you!"

Su Lin blushed. While she stood beside my wheelchair, I slipped my arm around her waist. Pointing to the sky, I said, "Someday I'll fly you up there into the wild blue yonder." She hugged my neck, and looking skyward, said, "I *rike* that!" I boldly hugged her back.

When we embraced, her hair became entangled in my dog tags as well as the St. Christopher medal I always wore. As we untangled her hair, she asked, "What this?" referring to the medal.

"This is a St. Christopher medal. St. Christopher is a Christian saint who protects travelers." I turn it over, "See, I even have my initials engraved on the back. So far, St. Christopher's done a good job protecting me."

"Like Buddha!" she chirped.

Not knowing how to explain the difference, I just let it go.

• • •

It's now well over six weeks since I've been in a cast and knowing my stay here in Wai Sang is coming to an end, I'm distressed at the thought of leaving Su Lin and rejoining the fleet. Fortunately, the decision is not mine to make. Dr. Míng Jié, in the course of conducting his daily examination, taps the plaster cast with his pen, and states, "I think it's time to remove the cast and see how you fare. You'll have to use crutches for a while, and it'll take some time for you to regain the strength in both of your legs and maybe even your arms. However, you're young and healthy so it shouldn't be too daunting."

When I hear the news, I experience mixed emotions. I'm homesick and eager to rejoin the Americans but saddened at the prospect of leaving Su Lin. "How long before I can get back to my ship?" I ask.

"As soon as we can arrange a transport. You have excellent Navy doctors assigned to the fleet. They can monitor your progress better than we can here." The doctor motions for Hóng to remove the cast. "I'm going to contact your commander and let him know you're good to go as soon as they can arrange for the pickup."

After the cast is removed, I shower and don fresh clothing. I feel like a new man. Using the crutches, I make my way back to my bed, where I find the doctor waiting for me.

"I have bad news, or good news, depending on how you look at it—" the doctor begins.

"Oh, no. Not more bad news," I blurt.

"Like I said, depending on how you look at it. It appears like you're going to spend another week with us," the doctor remarks. "Your commander didn't go into details, but I suspect the delay is because there's something brewing that is obviously top secret."

Another week! Something earth shattering it appears is about to happen. Wonder what it is and how the fleet fits in.

The doctor doesn't seem to notice my dilemma. He's standing at the foot of my bed scribbling on the chart. Without looking up, he comments, "We'll get you started on a rehab program in the interim." After a pause, he continues, "You may not know it, but you've become quite the celebrity here in our modest facility and you having shed your cast is common knowledge throughout the hospital. Your hospital fans, as well as our patients and personnel alike, applaud your recovery.

"And you'll be pleased to know when I passed the mess, as you call it, I noticed the cook preparing chow mein for dinner. Knowing how much you like his chow mein, he said it was to celebrate your recovery. You've captivated the hearts of many of us and we'll miss you when you leave."

Fighting with those damn tears again, I respond, "Doctor, I couldn't have asked for any better care. I'll miss you and the rest of the staff here at the hospital. My stay here has been an eye-opening experience and I'll carry fond memories of Wai Sang and especially the hospital staff with me for the rest of my life. Please convey my warmest thanks to my *fans* and let them know, at least in my opinion, they're the real heroes."

Dr. Míng Jié nods and replaces the chart on the rail at the foot of my bed. He then extracts a handkerchief from his pants pocket and dabs at his eyes. Avoiding my gaze, he says, "Allergies," and leaves the room. I, too, dab at my allergies after he closes my door.

Chapter Four

Together

The next morning when Su Lin arrives with the wheelchair for our morning stroll, she's surprised that my cast has been removed. "That good you use leg, yes?" she queries.

"Yes! I feel like a new man. However, it's going to take some therapy to regain the strength and normal use of both legs."

I watch Su Lin's face darken as she looks down. "This mean you leave Wai Sang soon?" I detect sadness in her voice.

Sharing her anguish, I remark, "Not for at least another week." I hobble over to the wheelchair and say, "Let's go to your bonsai garden."

Su Lin immediately brightens. "Oh, not *my* garden, belong to all."

I smile and nod. After helping me in to the wheelchair, she wheels me through the hospital corridors. Once we're outside, we catch sight of dense clouds and the threat of rain. Su Lin, always looking at the bright side, remarks, "Maybe we walk in rain today. That okay with you?"

"Absolutely! Used to play in the rain when I

was a kid. I love rainy days," I respond.

"Me, too," she smiles and continues to push the wheelchair.

Her comments remind me of a popular love song, so I plagiarize a few lyrics and sing to her as we proceed down the path toward the bonsai trees. "*We strolled the lane together, walked in the rain together, though you're gone from me, in my reverie, it always will be... your* bonsai garden that I see."

Su Lin giggles at my feeble attempt to imitate a crooner. "What mean reverie?" she asks as we approach the bonsai cul-de-sac.

I scratch my head trying to come up with just the right words. I want her to know how much she means to me, and this is a perfect opportunity. Mustering up the nerve, I say, "Reverie means memory, usually many happy memories. The times I've spent with you are some of my happiest memories. What I'm saying, Su Lin, is *you* are my happiness."

Su Lin stops pushing, and rounding the wheelchair, she kneels before me and grasps my hands in hers. Blushing, she whispers, "You my happiness, too."

There it is, right in my face. Cupid obviously has a distorted sense of humor. Piercing our hearts with his *poisoned* arrows at the twelfth hour does not amuse me. It's more like a sadistic joke.

Noticing the distress tattooed on my face, Su Lin asks, "What you thinking? I say something wrong?"

I pull her close and stroke her hair as I take a moment to organize my thoughts and the sudden rush of emotion I'm experiencing. I finally answer, "I'm thinking of how cruel war is and how many millions of lives have been destroyed or altered forever. Married couples torn apart, children who will never know their fathers, parents who have lost children and the promise of grandchildren—and for what? To satisfy the power mongers who want to control the world." By the look on her face, I can tell Su Lin is confused.

"My anguish is also for us. I want to take you in my arms, run away with you, and never let you go." Before she can say anything, I rush on. "But that's not the American way. I have an obligation to fulfill. The monsters who wage war must be eradicated." Taking her face in my hands, I gaze into her eyes, "I'd ask you to wait for me but that would be selfish on my part…"

Her arms are suddenly around my neck and her cheek presses against mine. Our tears mingle as she whispers, "I wait, I wait always."

As if on cue, thunder rattles the afternoon stillness and droplets of rain soon turn into a downpour. We're both laughing as Su Lin rushes us out of the garden and back inside the hospital, but not before we're completely soaked.

• • •

The week passes much too quickly, and this is my last night in Wai Sang. I'm eager to rejoin my squadron but despairing at the thought of leaving Su Lin. Before she leaves the hospital for the day, she stops by my room.

Standing close to my bedside, she takes my hand. "Tomorrow I come early. We go for last walk in garden."

I take both of her hands in mine, "Not *last walk*," I utter. "I love you and I *will* be back. Although I can't promise you more than that, I can guarantee nothing less." I then raise her hands to my lips and kiss them.

She squeezes my hands, "I love you, too." She then turns and rushes from the room, disappearing down the corridor.

• • •

I'm still on a regimen of nightly sleeping pills. After Hóng delivers mine, I scrunch down in bed, and am soon drifting into a restless slumber. It must've been sometime after midnight when I sense someone slip into bed beside me and the aroma of Su Lin's hair fills my nostrils. I'm only half awake and can't tell if the sensation is a euphoric dream or the real thing—I only know I don't want it to end. When I awake later that night, I find I'm alone in my bed, and wonder if the experience was nothing more than wishful thinking.

• • •

The sun is barely up when I'm rousted by Hóng. "Your plane on way," he announces.

I look at my watch. "But it's way too early," I protest.

"They fly clear sky," he explains. "Storm come later." With an anxious expression, he adds, "We must hurry!"

Su Lin! I won't get to say goodbye to Su Lin.

Hóng has my clothing laid out, so I quickly change into my uniform. I'm transported to the landing strip in a beat-up Jeep driven by Hóng, and we arrive just as one of the fighter jets from the fleet taxies to a halt.

Although Su Lin has no way of knowing about the sudden turn of events, I constantly turn my head looking for her hoping by some twist of fate she will show up so I can at least say goodbye.

Hóng drives me across the dusty runway to the plane but before I'm hoisted into the copilot seat, I remove my St. Christopher medal and hand it to him.

"Please give this to Su Lin," I shout over the roar of the jets. He nods and I get the feeling he understands the gesture is more than just a gift.

Chapter Five

You Belong to My Heart

I'm steadfastly committed to the cause of worldwide freedom and think of Su Lin every day and pray the village of Wai Sang has been spared. The war is still raging at the conclusion of my second four-year commitment, so I reenlist for the second time and am assigned to a carrier where I fly a Warhawk fighter jet.

Because of my love of flying, I'm seriously considering the twenty-five-year retirement option. When I finish this four-year reenlistment, I'm halfway there. The world is still at war and pilots are in great demand. However, planning *my* future is only one consideration. I want to marry Su Lin, and my hope is her feelings for me don't change during my absence.

• • •

Five years pass before I finally have an opportunity to make it back to China and the village of Wai Sang. During my hospitalization, I never knew where Su Lin lived, so I begin my search for her at the hospital. I'm delighted when the receptionist, Qu Lán, informs me that Dr. Míng

Jié still practices medicine there.

"I remember you," Qu Lán says and smiles. "I be here when you patient."

"That was a longtime ago," I comment. "Good memory!"

Qu Lán is all smiles when she escorts me to the interior of the hospital. When we arrive, she points, and I see Dr. Ming Jié standing at the nurse's station studying a chart. Noticing my presence, he turns and when he sees me, he closes the distance between us in three strides. Our handshake turns into a hug. "Captain Steven Parker!" he exclaims as he gently disengages, "You look fit as a fiddle. I must've done a crackup job on your leg."

"Fiddle, hell! More like a Stradivarius," I reply and tap my right leg with my captain's hat for emphasis. "However, I prefer not using the term *crackup*." We both chuckle. Then looking around the facility, I remark, "Nothing seems to have changed."

Setting his clipboard aside, the doctor muses, "Only on the inside. Our village escaped most of the physical destruction wreaked on our homeland. Sometimes being small potatoes has its advantages. Apparently, the Japanese didn't think Wai Sang was worth wasting a bomb. However, the war has ravaged many of our countrymen in various ways, leaving not only visible but invisible scars on most of us. The fallout was physical, mental, or emotional, and in some cases, all of the above. No one escaped unscathed."

How well I know. Not wanting to get into sharing war stories, I remark, "As good as it is to see you, my time is limited and I'm searching for someone. Does Su Lin still volunteer here?"

Suddenly, a sense of dread descends on me when, instead of immediately answering, the doctor passes the chart he was studying to the nurse behind the counter. "Come into my office," he says. I follow him to a small room just large enough for a desk and two chairs. He closes the door behind us and points me to a chair and takes a seat opposite me. There's an aura of gloom permeating the room. I don't like the way this feels but I wait patiently.

"I've had to do this way too many times over the span of my career," Dr. Míng Jié begins, "and it doesn't get any easier with the passage of time…" When he pauses, I stiffen anticipating the worst. He finally says, "Su Lin passed away several years ago."

I feel as though I've been struck on the head with a sledgehammer. "No! No! That can't be!" I hear someone bellow. It's only when the doctor puts his hand on my shoulder that I realize it was me doing the screaming. I double over as sobs rack my body. After a few moments, I take a deep breath and whimper, "What happened?"

"She hemorrhaged while giving birth and died soon after the child was born."

"Child?" I query.

"Yes. Nine months after you left, almost to the day, Su Lin gave birth to a baby boy."

"Nine months…" Memories of my last night in the hospital flood my brain. *The erotic encounter wasn't a dream after all!* I cover my face with my hands and slump back into the chair as I wrestle with my feelings. When the initial shock subsides, I put two and two together and realize I'm the father. "Wh…what happened to the child?" I stutter.

"Parker was a sturdy infant—" the doctor begins. I cut him off midsentence.

"Parker?"

"Yes. Su Lin lived long enough to hold the baby in her arms and name him." The doctor pauses before adding, "She died peacefully holding the infant—if that's any consolation."

I fight the urge to break down again when I realize she named our son after me, ignoring Chinese tradition.

The doctor continues as I struggle with my emotions. "Captain Parker, when Su Lin first suspected she was pregnant, she asked me to confirm her suspicions. It was during that examination that she confided in me that you were the father and the circumstances under which she became pregnant. She never blamed you and she made me promise I wouldn't disclose that you were the father to anyone. As far as I know, I'm the only one she told."

I sit in stunned silence as the doctor continues. "Of course, the baby had some Caucasian characteristics which made it plain that an American was the father. Chinese customs are very strict and especially upon those in prominent positions. Her father was still mayor at that time, and unable to hide the disgrace Su Lin brought down upon her family, and the child was rejected and eventually placed in an orphanage.

"Even though the orphanages were bulging with displaced children, I was able to keep track of him. Being half American, Parker was taunted by the other children in the facility. Although, he, of course, wasn't the only mixed breed in the orphanage, I, knowing his background, was concerned about his mental as well as his physical development and felt a sense of loyalty and that I owed it to Su Lin to intercede on his behalf. I used my connections and with the help of a fellow physician who practices at Walter Reed, I was provided with an avenue for

Parker to be sent to America to be schooled. I later learned that a childless Chinese couple, who had some years before migrated to the United States, adopted Parker. The only other bit of information I was privy to was that they live in Herndon, Virginia, and Parker attends school there."

Although I'm overwhelmed trying to absorb the events the doctor is relating, I nod and say, "I'm on leave and heading home to see my family in Georgia. Perhaps I could make a stop in Virginia on my way. I'd like to see Parker, if possible."

Dr. Míng Jié looks thoughtful. He finally says, "Even though it's a foregone conclusion that you're likely the biological father, it's highly unlikely you'd be allowed a visit unless the adoptive parents agree to it. Strict rules apply after adoption." After a pause, he continues, "But, like I said, I have connections. I'll see what I can do. I know Su Lin would want you to get to know your son." Rising from his chair, the doctor asks, "Where are you staying?"

Following his lead, I also rise. "The barracks at the airstrip."

"I know the commander there. Nice fellow. In the meantime, I'll make some calls to my contacts in the States and see if it can be arranged for you to visit your son."

"Thanks, doc," I say. "But with or without permission, I intend to see him. You see, I, too, have connections," and point to the expansive display of ribbons pinned to my military uniform.

"So, I see! And I would expect no less from you." We shake hands and he says as I turn to leave, "Oh, by the way, Captain, one of Su Lin's dying requests was that a St. Christopher medal she always wore be passed on to her son. I kept it for him for five years and just before he was picked up by his adoptive parents, I placed it around his neck." I watched tears gather in the doctor's eyes as he continued, "Amazingly, the boy seemed to understand that it was something special. He grasped the medal in his hand and pressed it to his heart."

Too choked up with grief to say anything, I just nod. We shake hands once again and I head for the hospital exit.

• • •

"Captain Parker! Captain Parker!" someone calls from behind me before I get to the door. When I turn, I recognize Hóng, the orderly who attended me when I was a patient here.

"Hóng!" I reply and extend my hand. He eagerly grasps it in both of his. "How have you been?" I ask.

"I be well, Captain." He then looks around before saying, "We talk!"

"Sure," I say, and wonder why all the secrecy.

"Not want all to hear. We go to garden?" he asks and points to the rear exit.

When he mentions the garden, I'm overcome with melancholy, remembering the private times I spent there with Su Lin. Steeped in guilt, I suddenly remember a priest once telling me, God forgives us so we must learn to forgive ourselves, especially for things we can't change. *Maybe I need one last visit for closure.* "Yes, I'd like that. Are the bonsai still thriving?"

"You see when we go there," he remarks.

We're silent as we proceed toward Su Lin's bonsai garden. Memories bombard me as we pass familiar landmarks, and my resolve is fading. I'm close to becoming emotional again by the time we reach the bonsai. Everything looks the same, but nothing feels the same. Hóng and I sit cross-legged on the grass facing the seven pillars that support the miniature trees.

Why did he bring me back here? Trying to sound casual, I say, "Someone has been taking good care of the trees."

"Chinese heritage. They get good care."

I nod. "So, what can I do for you, Hóng," I ask, not wanting to prolong the agony welling up inside me.

"I tell you secret. Only for you!" he replies and relates the following: "Wěi Qí, Su Lin father, find out about baby. He very mad! He say he not kill her but she must leave home and never come back."

"Oh, no!" I sob, unable to control my emotions any longer. "What happened to her?" I manage to ask.

"She disgrace family. No one help. Wai Sang people not want make mayor mad. When Doctor Míng Jié learn what father do, he get much mad. He search and find Su Lin. He bring her to hospital. She very weak. She not live long after baby come."

As if in a trance, I ask, "Where is she buried?"

"She no buried. Father very sad she die. He come take body and cremate." Hóng then looks around in a conspiratorial manner before continuing. "Mǎ Lee, Su Lin sister, know Su Lin love bonsai. After cremate, I see Mǎ Lee in garden. I watch. She take small jar from obi and empty on dirt in bonsai pot. I call her, 'What you do here?' She look 'fraid and cry. She tell me she put little bit Su Lin ashes on bonsai and she 'fraid someone see and tell father 'cause she break law. I tell her I no say something. She thank me and say, 'Now Su Lin live thousand years with bonsai tree.'"

"What? Her ashes are here?" I blurt.

"Only tiny bit. Mǎ Lee only put on one tree,"

Hóng says. "Ash good, no harm tree."

"Which tree?" I demand.

Hóng points to the tree in the middle. "Mǎ Lee know that one Su Lin like best," he says.

I'm stunned and so distraught, I can't think, much less talk.

"I hear you talk to doctor," Hóng says. "He not know what Mǎ Lee do, only me." Hóng looks around apparently making sure no one is overhearing our conversation. He then says, "Now you know." Hóng stands, and after ritualistically bowing, leaves.

I'm now alone in the bonsai garden with only memories of Su Lin and my sorrow to keep me company. A few minutes pass. I can't communicate with her physically, but I can spiritually so I begin, "I'm so sorry, Su Lin, please forgive me. I'll love you forever," I whisper as I swipe tears from my cheeks. "I will find our son and see that he is well taken care of, I promise you that." Just as I finish and am preparing to leave, a rose finch swoops from the sky toward the bonsai. I recognize it by its pink and gray feathers. It perches on the top branch of the middle tree and cocks its head looking at me as if it knows me. *Is this a sign from Su Lin?* I wonder.

Chapter Six

When Johnny Comes Marching Home

The war is over when the Axis alliance is destroyed. On May 7, 1945, after Hitler committed suicide, Germany surrendered. Italy surrendered two days later. However, Japan continued to fight although they were warned by the U.S. that they would face utter destruction if they didn't surrender. They stubbornly resisted threatening the U.S. with the loss of more American lives. Sadly enough, it took two atomic bombs to convince Japan to give it up. After Hiroshima and Nagasaki were destroyed, the Empire of Japan reluctantly surrendered on September 2, 1945. The number killed in the atomic bombings of Hiroshima and Nagasaki is thought to be less than three hundred thousand. By ending the war in the Pacific by bombing the Japanese cities of Hiroshima and Nagasaki, it's estimated that thirty million lives were saved by putting an end to the war. The math supports the decision.

• • •

Freedom rings around the globe and when our fleet docks in San Francisco harbor, we're transported from the carrier to the pier by a tender, more commonly known as a ferry. The pier is in utter chaos teaming with military returning home and civilians who come to meet them.

Husbands and wives, parents and children, sisters and brothers, friends, and lovers, all intermingle on the dock bubbling over with the joy of at last being reunited. I don't complain when I'm hugged and kissed by females I don't even know. Males shake my hand and pat me on the back as they express their gratitude for my service. Their exuberance is contagious, and it feels so great to be back in the States I even welcome the hustle and bustle. I shoulder my seabag and weave my way through the menagerie milling around on the pier, hoping to get clear of the overbearing crowd in one piece.

"Hey! Parker! Captain Parker!" I hear someone shout from behind me. I look around and see a sailor waving his arms above his head. I watch him push his way through the throng and when he gets close enough, I recognize him.

"Hank Mitchell! What the…" before I can finish, Hank has me in a bearhug. When he releases me, I step back and look him over. Recognizing the uniform he's wearing, I comment, "Looks like you joined the Seabees, after all."

"Damn straight!" he exclaims. "Serving my

country by doing what I love to do is the smartest thing I ever did. And look at you, you ol' war dog!" he says and points to the ribbons pinned to my uniform. "What are you doing in San Francisco?"

I motion to where the fleet is anchored, "Just got in," I reply. "And you?"

"Same. For how long?" he asks.

"Two-week furlough. And you?"

"Same. If you're at loose ends, let's go somewhere and grab a beer and catch up," he suggests.

"Lead the way!"

We flag down and board the bus headed for Fisherman's Wharf. Even though the bus is so crowded there's barely standing room, the driver stops and when he opens the door, we're pulled aboard by enthusiastic patriots who somehow make room for us. The camaraderie is uplifting. Those coming home, even if just on a short leave like Hank and me, appear to be so happy the war is over they can't contain their excitement and bellow the popular songs of the day. The current, and very appropriate choice is "When Johnny Comes Marching Home." The singing rocks the bus as we traverse Jefferson Street. There's something about music that binds humankind, and although I don't know all the lyrics, I sing along with the refrain—and it feels good. Hank, having shed his inhibitions, joins in the singing. Pedestrians wave and shout as the bus passes. There's a carnival-like atmosphere citywide and the bus driver is all smiles. Conversation is impossible so we just ride along singing and enjoying the celebration.

When we arrive at Fisherman's Wharf, my ears are ringing from the boisterous singing, but the ride is so uplifting, I don't mind. We debus, and Hank and I scour the pier. At a seafood restaurant, we stand in line twenty minutes before we're finally seated. However, the wait isn't all that bad since the owner comps the wait line with glasses of wine and mugs of beer to ease the pain of waiting.

Once we're seated, Hank spreads his napkin on his lap, and remarks, "I was beginning to think we were going to spend our entire furlough waiting for a table." He looks around. "I've been here a few times. It's worth the wait."

"Hank, you look great!" I exclaim. "What happened after you left China?"

"Well, as you noticed, I joined the Seabees, and after bootcamp, the journey began."

"I know about the Seabees but not specifically what they do. I'm interested in what you call your *journey*," I say, "so fill me in."

"Long story, but I'll give you the *Reader's*

Digest version—and some of this I didn't even know," Hank begins. "There are over three hundred and fifty thousand men enlisted in the Seabees which consists of a hundred and fifty-one naval construction battalions. The battalions are completely equipped and designed to be self-sustaining. Our talent is drawn from civilian heavy construction outfits and includes those who were involved in constructing dams, highways, skyscrapers, subway tunnels, docks, and wharfs just to mention a few. Our engineers are equipped to design and implement the construction of bridges and floating docks on the spot." Hank pauses and the pride is evident in his voice when he adds, "We were in every theatre during the war, and besides the building aspect, we engaged in fighting as well."

"Don't think many people realize that the Seabees were engaged in hand-to-hand combat," I say.

"Best kept secret in town," Hank says. Then with a broad smile, he adds, "It's a little-known fact, but the Seabees are the highest paid outfit in the military."

"What? I didn't know that. Being a snobby jet jockey, I thought we were."

"I know," Hank retorts, and as he raises his beer mug in salute, he says, "Dinner's on me!"

A waiter takes our order and after he retreats, Hank remarks, "Looks like the leg mended and you've returned to duty. It's been a while since I last saw you. What's new with you?"

"I'll return the favor and also give you the *Reader's Digest* version," I say. "Before returning to the States, I stopped over in Wai Sang. The village escaped virtually unharmed, and the hospital is still operating and not just literally. Dr. Míng Jié and Hóng are still there, and everything appears to be as it was when we were patients."

"How 'bout Su Lin?" Hank asks as he pops a hushpuppy into his mouth.

I take a swig from my beer mug and shake my head. Hank must've noticed my destress. After an awkward moment, he prompts me. "What is it?"

Taking a deep breath, I wrestle with my emotions. When I'm finally able to speak, I fill Hank in on everything that transpired after he left Wai Sang, including the baby, the circumstances surrounding the birth, and what Dr. Míng Jié told me about the adoption. When I explain to Hank that I'm on a quest to locate my son, he exclaims, "Let me help you find him!"

I'm surprised Hank wants to spend his furlough helping me search for my son and I say so.

"It's personal," Hank remarks. "You recall, I

was adopted and never knew who my biological parents were despite numerous attempts to find them. When I was younger not knowing haunted me, and truthfully, I still dream of finding them someday."

"I'm sorry," I say. "I should have remembered. And yes, Hank, I'd be grateful for your help." After a pause, I add, "Don't have a clue on how or where to begin." After a moment, I add, "Any ideas?"

"Well, having some history of trying to find my own parents, I do have some ideas. And you, at least, have the major advantage of a starting place. Very fortunate the doctor mentioned Herndon, Virginia. That obviously should be our first stop."

Hank's exuberance inspires me, and despite the odds, I'm now more optimistic about the prospects. However, I can't help but feel it's still like trying to find a needle in a haystack.

• • •

After dinner, we check with the airlines. Those returning home from the war have impacted the industry and we're told there's a five-day waiting list for flight reservations. We decide to take the train. Herndon is only twenty-five miles from D.C. The train trip from San Francisco to Washington, D.C. takes two days and it's better than standing in line at the airport, so we purchase train tickets and are soon on our way. All the cars are full of returning military and the end of the war celebration rivals that of the San Francisco bus ride to Fisherman's Wharf. The uproar on the train lasts the entire two days and is a welcome distraction.

• • •

Exhausted from lack of sleep, and all the celebrating, we arrive in Washington at three in the morning and luckily find a hotel with a vacancy. My bed is lumpy and uncomfortable but that doesn't keep me from falling asleep. I don't wake up until eight the following morning.

We have breakfast at a nearby diner, and afterwards, Hank suggests our first stop should be the library. When Hank inquires what would be the best source for determining populations, a friendly librarian retrieves the American Fact Finder and escorts us to a reading table. We thank her and once we're seated, Hank conducts research of Herndon, Virginia. Whispering, he reads: "Herndon, Virginia, is considered to be part of the Washington, D.C. metropolitan area and has a population of approximately seventeen thousand."

Still keeping his voice low, he remarks, "So far lady luck is favoring us. The smaller the population, the better chance we have of finding your son." We rise, and returning the book to its shelf, we quietly exit the library.

Back in our hotel room, Hank suggests we use the phonebook to research Asian last names in Herndon. We underline the Asian last names and come up with just a few hundred. Things are looking up and I'm beyond encouraged. Taking the phonebook with us, we search for payphones. When we pass a bank, I stop and buy several rolls of nickels. Continuing our search, we pass the bus station and spot a bank of payphones.

"If we double up, we can get this done much faster," Hank suggests.

I agree and we enter the bus station and place the phonebook on the counter between us. Hank works his way forward while I start on the last page and work my way through the back half of the phonebook. Hank worked up a spiel for us to use so as not to alarm the person on the other end of the line. Approximately forty-five minutes into the process, we luck out and hit a homerun.

I ask, "Is this the Zhēn residence?"

"Yes, this is Chi Zhēn," a woman answers with a slight Chinese accent. "Who's calling please?"

Ignoring her question, I forge ahead, "Do you have a son named Parker?"

"Yes, Parker is our son. Why do you ask? Is anything wrong?" she demands and the anxiety in her voice is palpable.

"No! Didn't mean to alarm you. Nothing is wrong," I assure her. I nudge Hank, and holding the receiver so Hank can also hear the conversation, I tell her who I am and gave her a summary of my mission.

When I finish, she asks still sounding alarmed, "You want to take our boy?"

"No! No, nothing like that," I say. "I just want to meet him."

After a long silence, Mrs. Zhēn replies in a less stressed tone of voice, "I understand. The war was a terrible thing. Many families were torn apart. We, me and my husband, Niàn, escaped China when the Japanese invaded. We fled to America seeking asylum. After getting established here, we adopted Parker."

When she pauses, I ask, "Mrs. Zhēn, I've never met my son and I'm curious as to what made you choose Parker out of all of the thousands of orphans?"

"I prefer to be called Chi," she says. "It's less formal." She hesitates momentarily, then continues, "I understand, and if I was in your place, I, too, would be curious. So, to answer your question, there were so many children refugees flooding into the country, it was certainly a difficult decision. Since we wanted a boy about five or six years old, the list was narrowed but still daunting. We were provided grainy photographs of eligible boys in our age range. After studying them for hours, we, Niàn and I that is, kept going back to Parker's photo. His bright eyes and cheerful expression captivated our hearts.

"We had pretty much decided on Parker, and when we learned Parker's biological father was American and his mother Chinese, it was like a sign from God. You see, his heritage represents both of our countries, China and now America."

I'm touched by Chi's narration and sophistication and can now relax since I feel Parker is in good hands.

"Would you allow me to meet him?" I ask.

When she hesitates, I fear the answer will be no. She finally says, "Niàn is at work and Parker is in school. I don't think Niàn would object to you meeting Parker, but I must first get Niàn's approval. Since tomorrow is Saturday and both Niàn and Parker will be home, call me tomorrow morning and I'll have an answer for you."

I thank Chi and hang up the phone. Hank's grinning from ear-to-ear.

"Congratulations! Against all odds, you found him!" Hank bellows.

"Not me, *we* found him—and Sherlock, it

was mostly your detective work that did it!" I retort. "I never cease to be impressed with your resourcefulness."

Ignoring my compliment, Hank says, "Come on, buddy, we gotta do some shopping," and he pulls me toward one of the exits of the bus station where several outgoing buses are standing.

"What are we shopping for?" I ask.

"You'll see," he replies.

• • •

We take a crosstown bus to the downtown area and exit across the street from a Woolworths. Hank, more of a daredevil than me, dodges the heavy traffic as we jaywalk amid blaring horns and berserk drivers who yell obscenities. I'm amazed we made it to the other side of the street in one piece. *And I thought air-to-air combat was dangerous.* We find refuge in the store. Once inside, I'm overwhelmed because the store is so well stocked.

"What exactly are we looking for?" I ask as my curiosity is piqued.

"A gift for your son. My nephews love their Lincoln Logs," Hank says. "They're educational and challenging—not to mention intriguing."

"Of course, they are!" I smirk. "Since their uncle is a builder, why wouldn't they be intrigued? Subjecting them to undue influence, hardly seems fair."

"Ahh, you think?" Hank shoots back.

The store is immense, and it's not an easy task to find the toy department or even an employee to direct us. When at last we accidently stumble upon the toy department, the latest version of Lincoln Logs has just been restocked. Hank grabs a box and tucks it snugly under his arm.

Judging by the way Hank cradles the box, you'd think there was going to be a run on Lincoln Logs. As I turn toward the front of the store, preparing to leave, Hank stops me.

"Hold on, partner," he says. "We're not finished shopping yet." He drags me into the sports section and I watch him rummage through the stacks of paraphernalia finally selecting a Virginia Cavaliers visor cap.

"The Virginia Cavaliers are Virginia's major league football team. Even if Niàn isn't a football fan, I think he'll like this one," Hank says and holds up a navy-blue cap with a large white V on the front underscored by two crisscrossed red sabers.

Although still impressed, I'm also perplexed. "How'd you know all of this?" I ask.

"Elementary, my dear Watson. T*he Richmond Daily* was lying open on the counter this morning at the diner where we had breakfast. The headlines read 'Cavaliers continue march toward World Championship playoffs.' Two and two still add up to four," Hank says, flashing me his patented grin.

Having my feathers singed twice, and since women are so hard to buy for, I'm hoping to regain some dignity by stumping him with a gift for Chi. I ask, "Okay, smart guy, what do you suggest we get Chi?"

Without missing a beat, Hank responds, "Candy! Name me one woman who wouldn't love a box of chocolates. I'd even like that!"

Once again, I come up the loser and am embarrassed that I even challenged him. Standing in line at the checkout counter, *I think, Thank God for Hank. What a great idea. I wouldn't have thought of bringing gifts—much less have his insight into what gifts would be the most appropriate.*

When we exit Woolworths, Hank's toting a shopping bag containing our purchases. It's late afternoon, and looking up and down the street, Hank comments, "I'm starved. Let's find somewhere nice for dinner. You tired of seafood?"

"Hell no!" I reply. "Anything but mystery meat and blueberry surprise."

"You've got to quit eating at the mess halls!" he says.

We find a nice restaurant and arrive early enough

to avoid the dinner rush. The aroma of a medley of food permeates the dining room exciting my senses and my mouth begins to water. Everything on the menu looks tempting and I wallow in indecision.

Our waiter brings a small basket of hushpuppies along with the mugs of beer we ordered. Hank looks up from his menu and tells the waiter he'd like the captain's seafood platter. What the heck? Sounds good to me so I order the same.

In less than fifteen minutes, the waiter places platters heaped with lobster, crab legs, and deep-fried shrimp accompanied by mounds of French-fries and a variety of condiments before us.

I gasp when I see the amount of food we're served and look at the waiter. "Compliments of the management," he says. "In gratitude for your service. Welcome home, gentlemen!"

An hour later when we waddle from the restaurant, I groan as I say to Hank, "I'm so stuffed, I may never eat again."

"You'll get over it," he replies.

• • •

The next morning, after having a light breakfast at the diner, I telephone Chi.

"Hello," she answers. When I identify myself, she replies, "Captain Parker, when I told Niàn about you and your request, he said he fully understood and would be honored to have you come to our home and meet Parker."

"That's wonderful," I exclaim. "When can we come?"

"We? Are you with someone?" Chi asks.

"Yes. A fellow serviceman who helped me locate you and Niàn."

Chi must've covered the mouthpiece because all I can hear is muffled sounds in the background. A few moments later Chi's back on the line. "You're both welcome," Chi says, and without hesitation adds, "Please join us for lunch around noon."

"Thank you, Chi. We'll be there," I reply.

After I hang up, Hank punches me on the bicep. "Score!" he bellows and raises his arms in the universally recognized touchdown signal.

I fade back, imitating a quarterback getting ready to throw a pass. Hank runs a few paces up the avenue. Then turning back, he jumps up and catches the imaginary ball.

Pedestrians stare at us as they move past. One elderly gentleman stops and says, "Welcome home, sirs!" Then pointing to himself he remarks, "WW I, Battle of Belleau Wood, 1919."

We both salute him; he returns our salute.

• • •

Hank and I take a taxi to the Zhēn residence

and arrive a few minutes before noon. I study the premises through the cab's window as I pay the driver. The house looks to be above average, and the lawn is well kept. When I step from the vehicle, I'm awash with emotion not knowing what to expect. My greatest fear is that Parker won't like me.

Hank is standing on the walkway. "Come on, buddy," he encourages and starts toward the front door. When I don't move, he looks back, "You want me to carry you?"

"What if—" I say.

Hank cuts me off. "Life is full of what ifs! And in this case, you'll never know if you don't get the lead out."

I nod, wave the cab on, and join Hank.

Apparently the Zhēns have been watching from their bay window. Suddenly the front door flies open and a child races across the lawn in our direction. He's a handsome lad with dark hair and tawny skin. His eyes are brown but more American in shape than Chinese and he appears to be the normal size for a six-year-old. He pauses when he reaches us, and I go down on one knee and put out my hand. Much to my delight, he ignores my hand and jumps into my embrace wrapping his arms tightly around my neck.

"Daddy Steven," he says as he hugs me. Niàn

and Chi must've prepared him before we arrived. I try to control my emotions but can't as I caress the boy. Su Lin's and my son! After a few moments, Parker gently pulls away and looks up at Hank. That gives me a chance to dry my tears.

Hank extends his hand, "I'm Daddy Steven's friend, Hank, and I'm pleased to meet you."

Parker smiles broadly and gingerly shakes Hank's hand. "Pleased to meet you, too," he says.

By this time the Zhēns have joined our group. After introductions all around, we walk to the house. Hank is carrying the shopping bag that contains the gifts. Once we're inside, he hands it to me and winks. I get the message—this is my show!

Chi directs us into the living room. "You all relax and get acquainted while I finish lunch," she says and turns to leave.

Before she gets too far away, I say, "Wait, Chi. I have something for you," and pull the fancy box of chocolates from the shopping bag and hand it to her.

"Oh, my!" Chi exclaims excitedly. She then looks at Niàn, apparently seeking approval to accept the gift.

I notice the gesture and quickly remove the Cavalier cap from the shopping bag and hand it to Niàn. "And this is for you," I announce.

A broad smile crosses Niàn's face as he accepts

the cap. He immediately puts it on. "How do I look?" he asks.

"Like the number one fan of the next world champs," Hank says, and we all share a laugh.

Parker sits quietly on the sofa taking in the festivities. If he feels dejected, it doesn't show. I motion him to my side and take the Lincoln Logs from the bag. "And these are for you," I say. Then remembering my place, I add, "if your mom and dad approve."

"Oh, boy!" Parker shouts and looks at Niàn and Chi. "May I keep them?" he asks.

Niàn takes the lead. "I'm sure going to keep my Cavalier's cap and I don't think we could pry the chocolates away from your mother even if we tried. So yes, son, you may keep the gift."

No sooner said than done. Parker plops down on the floor, pries open the box, and dumps its contents out onto the living room carpet. When I look over at Hank, it's obvious he can't resist the urge. I nod and Hank sits down on the floor with Parker and begins assembling the logs. We watch as Hank shows Parker a few tricks he obviously learned from his nephews. The two are becoming fast buddies.

Within a short time after Chi leaves, she's back announcing that lunch is ready. Niàn and I stand

and start toward the dining room. I look back. Hank and Parker are still engrossed in connecting Lincoln Logs. I clear my throat and Hank apparently gets the message.

"Come on, Parker," Hank says. "We're holding up the show." The two of them suspend their project and join us.

Lunch is totally American—hot dogs and apple pie. As I smear mustard on my second dog, I ask Chi, "How'd you know these were our favorites?"

Chi blushes. "Hot dogs are everyone's favorite," she chirps. "We've been in America long enough to know that. Besides, they're easy to fix on a moment's notice."

"Well," says Hank, "your apple pie is as good as any I've ever eaten."

"Oh, my," Chi exclaims. "Would you like another slice?"

Hank holds out his empty pie plate in reply.

• • •

After lunch, Chi busies herself with clearing the dishes, Hank and Parker resume their building project and Niàn invites me to join him on the patio. The afternoon is serene, and we sit in padded chairs at a glass top table beside the swimming pool.

"Thank you for allowing me to meet my son," I say. "I was told that adoption records are pretty much inaccessible and finding an adopted child would be nothing short of impossible."

"Ah! And you found us, thus demonstrating perseverance, which is a good trait," Niàn says.

"I can't take credit," I reply. "Hank is the super sleuth. Couldn't have done it without his help."

"He seems like a fine fellow," Niàn comments.

"That he is," I say.

"We, Chi and I, witnessed so much human misery while living in China, we feel it's our duty to perform any act of kindness we can to offset the devastation the war left in its wake. Besides, as you can imagine, we're curious about Parker's lineage. All we were told when we adopted him was that his mother was Chinese and died giving birth and his father was an American serving in the military."

Since it appears Niàn is sincere in wanting to know about Parker's biological parents, I tell him the entire story leaving nothing to the imagination. I even tell him about the bonsai. He sits and listens without interrupting, only occasionally nodding or shaking his head as the circumstances dictate.

At the conclusion of my story, he says, "That explains a lot, including the origin of the St. Christopher medal Parker refuses to take off. Without being told, he must somehow sense it's a link to his past." We sit in silent reflection for a few moments. Niàn eventually says, "Parker asks about his real parents from time to time. Since he has had the opportunity to meet you in person, I wonder if you wouldn't mind telling him more about his mother if the opportunity presents itself."

"Of course," I say. "It appears he has inherited many of his mother's features and mannerisms." Then, reflecting on the time I spent with Su Lin, I add, "I have many happy memories of Su Lin that I'd like nothing more than to share with him."

Niàn glances toward the house then back at me. "Come, I want to show you something."

He escorts me to a gazebo with a pagoda-style roof positioned at the far end of the back lawn. When we enter, I see three bonsai trees positioned on the wooden railing which surrounds the gazebo. "You see, many Chinese share Su Lin's love for bonsai. My ancestors started these trees many, many years ago. Chi and I brought them to America when we migrated. We're training Parker on how to care for the cherished bonsai."

The expanse of lawn, the pagoda-style gazebo, and the bonsai take me back to the garden at the hospital where I spent many hours with Su Lin. I fight with the melancholy that threatens to overwhelm me and wish with all my heart Su Lin could see our son. "I've been fascinated with bonsai ever since Su Lin introduced me to them," I say as I study the three sturdy trees.

"Ah! It's difficult not to be mesmerized by them," Niàn replies. "Who would've thought one could keep a tree alive in such a small container for hundreds of years?" Then, looking thoughtful, he continues. "In ancient China, the art of bonsai was practiced only by the elite. In fact, the trees were so revered, they were given as special gifts and considered a luxury."

When we return to the patio, I say to Niàn, "Now you know my story, how about yours?"

After a long pause, Niàn nods. "Yes, you have the right to know, and you should." He points to the chair I previously occupied. He sits across from me, removes a pack of cigarettes from his breast pocket and holds the pack out to me. I shake my head. After he lights his cigarette, he begins. "Chi and I worked for the Chinese government before the Japanese invasion in 1937. Because of our jobs, we were privy to information not available to the public, and putting two and two together, we knew that a Japanese invasion was imminent. We were lucky enough to be forewarned, so to speak, so we pulled up roots and fled to America before there was a moratorium.

"We both were well educated and spoke fluent

English. In fact, both Chi and I made extra money tutoring government officials in our homeland and writing letters for them in English. With our language skills we were able to find work in the Chinatown district in New York, where we lived until we could relocate. Through a network of social workers, we eventually found work in Herndon and were able to buy a small house. As property values increased, we traded up, and after several years, ended up with this house." He paused and the pride in his eyes was unmistakable. "This is our dream home, and we like it here," he says. "To get Chi to move would be like taking a fish out of water."

"It's a lovely home," I comment.

"Thank you." He smiles and grinds the cigarette out in the ashtray on the table. Then he says, "Chi longed for a child, and since we were unable to have children of our own, we went through the legal process to adopt a Chinese child. Needless to say, it was a long, tedious task. However, after months of agonizing over the outcome, we were approved for the adoption.

"It was a sentimental journey when we traveled back to China to pick up our son. He was five at the time. The country had been ravaged by war and it saddened us to see the destruction of places where we lived not that long ago. When we arrived at the orphanage, we found, that because of so many applications from Americans wanting to adopt, the official in charge of the facility very wisely insisted the children be taught English as well as Chinese to make the transition smoother for both the adoptee and the adopting parents. Even though English is the major language spoken here in our household, we continue to educate Parker in the use of the Chinese language. Being bilingual certainly has its advantages in today's world. We want him to be proud of his heritage—both sides!

"Since the time he came into our lives, Parker's been the center of our world. He's a well-behaved child, his grades are above average, and he has a slew of friends. In fact, they're usually over here on the weekends taking advantage of the pool and Chi's treats."

When Niàn pauses, I say, "I'm grateful it was a couple like you and Chi that adopted Parker. Sometimes adoption doesn't work out too well. Here, it's a natural fit and Parker is fortunate to be so blessed."

"We, too, were blessed," Niàn replies.

I nod. "What do you do here in Herndon?"

Reaching for another cigarette, Niàn replies, "Still work for the government. With so many Orientals migrating to America, there's a demand for English-Chinese speaking people. I have a position with the Herndon court system as an official interpreter of the Chinese language."

Suddenly, I notice movement out of the corner of my eye and when I look around, I see Hank and Parker headed towards us walking hand in hand.

"How'd the building project go?" I ask when they're close enough.

"Parker's a natural!" Hank says with pride and grins down at Parker.

"Uncle Hank showed me how to build a cabin with the Lincoln Logs," Parker chirps.

"Uncle Hank, is it?" I mimic, trying not to sound jealous even though I am. My concern vanishes when Parker rushes up and hands me a small balsa-wood model airplane.

"Uncle Hank told me you fly planes," Parker remarks. "This is for you! I made it myself."

"You did!" I exclaim. And resist the urge to give him a hug remembering how embarrassed I was when my relatives hugged me when I was a kid. I examine the plane, and say, "It looks just like the ones I fly, only better." Parker rewards me with a wide toothy grin and an embrace that brings tears to my eyes.

I see myself in him and also Su Lin. Not sure which one of us he favors most. Su Lin would be most proud of our boy! I fight to hold back the tears, and Hank once again comes to the rescue. Looking at his watch, he asks, "Are you about ready? If so, I'll call a taxi."

Before I can respond, Niàn interrupts, "No need for a cab," he says. "I'll give you two a ride back to your hotel." Then looking at Parker, he adds, "We'll take Parker with us."

• • •

On the ride to our hotel, Niàn asks, "How long will the two of you be staying here in Herndon?"

"Not very long," I reply. "Flying back to San Fran is definitely not an option. There's a five-day waiting list. We'll probably take the train early Monday."

"In that case, will the two of you join us tomorrow for Sunday dinner? If you accept, I'll pick you up at eleven." He then adds, "Chi and you know who," Niàn nods toward Parker, "will be disappointed if you refuse."

I start to answer, but Hank beats me to it. "Thank you, but I've some old friends I should look up before I leave, so I'll pass—"

"Not on your life," I protest knowing Hank is making the concession for my benefit. "Your old friends can wait." Then to Niàn I say, "We'll both be ready at eleven tomorrow."

"Wonderful!" Niàn exclaims. "I have extra swim trunks, and we can take a dip after dinner."

"Oh boy!" Parker shouts and to Hank and me, he says, "Bet I can stay under water longer than either of you!"

"You're on!" I say. Meeting my son has been an answer to a prayer. Saying goodbye is not something I'm eager to do. I'm braced to do so but pray it won't be forever.

• • •

"What's all this malarkey about looking up old friends?" I ask when Hank and I are alone in our hotel room. "Since you never mentioned having and any friends here, much less old friends, I believe you're spoofing mainly for my benefit!"

Looking sheepish, Hank replies, "Aw, just wanted to give you some private time with family, that's all."

"Well, in case you haven't noticed, Uncle Hank is just as much family as Daddy Steven. Then after a pause, I add, "I confess I'm a bit jealous when I watch you and Parker interact. I'm still somewhat clumsy in my approach, but I'm learning. Apparently, you're a natural and kids gravitate to you."

Hank studies his fingernails for a few moments, then finally replies. "Your reaction is normal after all you've been through. Just for the record, I'd never do anything to undermine or hurt you. That's not how friends treat friends!" he responds. "And in case you haven't noticed, daddy trumps uncle every time!"

"Checkmate!" I say, then add, "Wanna grab a beer?"

"Damn straight. Thought you'd never ask."

I can tell Hank is avoiding eye contact to spare me embarrassment. Hank has been more of a brother to me than a friend. Without him and his insight, social skills, and patience, the visit with my son would have been a dismal failure, assuming it would ever have occurred.

• • •

Sunday morning, Hank and I are waiting in the lobby as Niàn pulls up in front of the hotel right on schedule. Parker sits next to him. When we pile into the car, Parker is all smiles. "Mother has a surprise for you," he says in a conspiratorial tone.

"Parker!" Niàn warns. "Don't spoil Mother's surprise."

Parker flushes and sinks back, staring out the window. It's obvious his feelings are hurt at the reprimand, so I attempt to lessen the pain by asking him, "Where do you go to school?"

He perks up when I mention school. "I go to George Washington. The school is named for our first president and it's so close to our house I can even walk by myself. My favorite classes are social studies and PE."

"Social studies!" I exclaim, "That was my favorite subject, too." I'm now feeling pretty good about being able to forge a bond with Parker. Recalling my discussion with Hank, I ask, "What's your favorite sport?"

"Basketball!" he answers without hesitation. "Dad hung a basketball basket on the garage. Maybe we could shoot a few…"

"I'd like that," I say and ruffle his hair.

Parker ducks his head and attempts to smooth his hair back into place. However, he's now all smiles. Apparently, he's forgotten about the hurt feelings.

• • •

When we enter the Zhēn residence, the aroma of fried chicken permeates the air. Chi meets us in the foyer. "I wanted to surprise you with my patented version of the all-American Sunday fried chicken dinner, but it appears the aroma of frying chicken more or less gave it away."

"It's still a delightful surprise and reminds me of home," Hank remarks. "My mouth is watering, and I can't wait to sink my teeth into a drumstick."

Thank God for Hank. He always comes to

the rescue. Without him, I'd be even more of a bumbling idiot!

Parker takes my hand and leads me into the dining room to a rectangular table with five place settings. "This is your seat," he says and pulls the chair out for me. He then takes the seat to my right. Niàn is seated at the head of the table, with Hank and Chi seated across from Parker and me. Glancing around the table, I conclude that we look like one of Norman Rockwell's Americana paintings.

The all-American dinner consists of southern fried chicken, mashed potatoes, cream gravy, steamed asparagus, buttermilk biscuits and homemade ice cream. I'm touched that Chi went to all the trouble to please us and I tell her so. She blushes and looks down. Niàn reaches across the table and squeezes her hand.

• • •

After dinner, Parker mentions swimming. Hank begs off saying his Navy career provides him enough contact with water. Chi also declines and retires to the kitchen to do the dishes. Niàn invites Hank into his den to listen to the world news broadcast on the radio. It's apparent they've all conspired to give me time alone with Parker and I'm grateful.

After changing into a pair of swim trunks

I borrowed from Niàn, Parker and I head for the pool. When he removes his T-shirt, I notice the St. Christopher medal suspended around his neck. "That's a nice medal," I say.

"Thank you. It was my mother's, my real mother's," he says and holds the medal up for me to have a closer look.

"I know," I respond. "I gave it to her the day I left Wai Sang. See, these are my initials here on the back," I say as I turn the medal over.

"I never knew that," Parker says as he wraps a beach towel around his shoulders but not without first examining the initials.

We sit side by side on the edge of the pool dangling our feet in the water and remembering Niàn's request that I tell Parker about his mother, I start to tell him about the Su Lin I knew and loved.

"You have many of your mother's characteristics," I say and begin by describing her and telling him how much he resembles her. "Your mother had long, silky black hair and warm brown eyes much like yours, except yours are shaped more like mine. She was gentle and caring and loved everything in nature, especially the bonsai trees.

"I met your mother after my plane crashed close to Wai Sang, your mother's village, at the beginning of the war. Your mother volunteered in the small hospital in Wai Sang and took special care of me. I had a broken right leg and a concussion. She made sure I took my medicine and she brought me my meals. Almost every day, she helped me into my wheelchair and pushed me out into the sunlight and through the garden behind the hospital. She's the one who introduced me to the bonsai trees. She told me they were her favorite—"

"We have bonsai!" Parker interrupts and looks toward the gazebo. "Daddy Niàn is teaching me how to care for them."

"I know. He showed them to me earlier," I say. Before I can say more, I hear the creak of the sliding patio door opening and watch as Chi, Niàn and Hank head in our direction. I breathe a sigh of relief. The sentimental journey and memories of Su Lin is taking its toll and I am close to an emotional breakdown—something I don't want to have happen in front of Parker.

Before Chi, Niàn and Hank get to the pool where we're seated, Parker frowns and asks in a sad voice, "Why do you have to leave?"

I'm elated. *He wants me to stay!* "Don't have a choice," I answer. "Otherwise, I would stay. My furlough is ending and I'm due back on the carrier by the end of the week." When I notice the dejected look on Parker's face, I quickly add, "You can bet

I'll stay in touch, and I'll be thinking of you every day. In fact, I'm going to hang the plane you gave me in the cockpit of my fighter jet. It'll be my good luck charm." Parker's broad smile replaces the frown.

Chapter Seven

We'll Meet Again

Since the war is over and the demand for combat pilots has dwindled, I'm assigned as a training officer based in Charleston, South Carolina. Parker and I frequently exchange letters, and I vicariously "watch" him grow up through reading his replies. Occasionally, I'm blessed with a phone call. Charleston is only an eight-hour drive from Herndon, and at the request of the Zhēns, I spend most major holidays with them. Each time I see Parker, I marvel at how much he has grown between visits and remember my mother saying that my brothers and I would outgrow our clothes so fast they were hand-me-downs before she could get the price tags removed.

Uncle Hank and I are also invited to participate in the significant milestones in Parker's life. We attended his grammar school graduation, his high school graduation, his college graduation, and today he is graduating at the top of his class from Harvard School of Law. However, Uncle Hank, because of a conflict, unfortunately, had to decline. Knowing Hank's propensity for making excuses so as not to interfere with family gatherings, I made him swear the conflict was legit. I reminded him of his Baptist upbringing and expounded on the consequences of hell's fire and eternal damnation if he lied. Rolling his eyes, he swore he was telling the truth and I reluctantly let him off the hook.

• • •

I sit in the auditorium alongside the Zhēns and reflect on the events that brought us to this time and place. My reverie is interrupted when the dean of the law school introduces Parker as valedictorian of his class. The attendees applaud and cheer and I'm astounded at Parker's popularity and poise when he takes the podium. How I wish Su Lin could be here to witness our son in all his glory as he gives the following address:

My fellow graduates, I'm beyond honored to be valedictorian of this amazing class of sixty-six. Today, I want to express my interpretation of the meaning of life and salute my parents who are here today. All four of them. Yes, four! You see, I'm one of the lucky few to have had two sets of parents. Even though my biological mother died giving me life, I feel her spiritual presence here at one of the most important events of my life. My biological father who is present in person today entered the Navy at the beginning of World War II and devoted twenty-five years of his life fighting for the freedoms we take for granted.

My adoptive parents migrated to America in the forties. They left the life they knew behind to start a new and hopefully better life here in our great country, a country full of promise and hope. They chose me to love and raise and be a part of their life. I am grateful to God for having placed them in my life along with my biological parents. Without the four of them I would not be standing here before you today.

My point is our lives are all interconnected. When we band together for the good of all, life is better for all. In the future, when we take, and hopefully pass, the bar exam, each of us will be sworn to support the Constitution of the United States. The same United States that those who have gone before us gave their lives to secure—life, liberty, and happiness for generations to come. We're all fortunate to be living in America and enjoying the American way of life.

I now conclude with my sincere wish that your hard work pays off and that your future is all you expect it to be when you hang that sheepskin above your desk. I pray that God blesses you as you carry on a hallowed career and tradition and may God bless America.

Couldn't be prouder of Parker. I'm not even embarrassed by the tears which refuse to be suppressed. I look over at Niàn and Chi. Tears also cascade down their cheeks. Chi glances at me, "Happy tears," she whispers. I nod.

• • •

The after-graduation ceremony is held in the stadium. The stands are awash with family, friends, alumni, faculty, and under classmates sporting Harvard's colors. Niàn, Chi, and I search the crowd for Parker, and just as we're about to give up, he finds us.

"There you are!" he exclaims as he rushes up to greet us. The excitement is evident in his voice. After hugs and handshakes all around, Parker asks, "I was pretty nervous when I gave my speech— how'd I do?"

Chi takes the lead. "We all cried," she says. "Tears of joy," she adds.

"Even Dad…. both of 'em?" Parker asks.

"Especially your dads," Chi says.

The bedlam encompassing the stadium as the graduates join up with family and friends makes it difficult to converse. We're constantly interrupted by well-wishers offering their congratulations and praise on Parker's address and many accomplishments. After about twenty minutes of chaos, Parker suggests we go someplace special for dinner.

As we leave the stadium, Parker says, "Since this is such an extraordinary occasion, I took the liberty of making reservations at the Hollingsworth. However, this ones on me. After all, I'm almost a full-fledged lawyer. Besides, I have something important I want to discuss with all of you."

"Hmm! Sounds like a bribe to me," I tease.

"Not even!" Parker scolds and accentuates his remark by giving me a punch on the bicep. "Just a pittance to express my gratitude and appreciation for all you three have done for me."

On the ride to the restaurant, Niàn and Chi seem to be very calm and relaxed, exhibiting more patience than yours truly. *Must be a Chinese trai*t. Curiosity gnaws at me and I'm on pins and needles waiting to hear what Parker has on his mind. *Is he going into the JAG Corp, interning with a law firm, hanging out his own shingle, joining the French Foreign Legion, getting married...?*

Once we're seated at the Hollingsworth and place our order, we all look at Parker with curious eyes. Taking the hint, Parker clears his throat and proceeds. "I've had a very unique and intriguing job offer," he begins. "An envoy from the office of the Secretary of Defense recently paid two of my classmates and me a visit. One of the classmates, Ivan Procoff speaks fluent Russian and the other, Cheyn Hoser, speaks fluent Vietnamese.

"As you know, the Department of Defense oversees the military forces needed to stave off war and protect America and American interests at home and abroad. It appears the War Department is looking for college graduates with law degrees and what they describe as exceptional language skills to help monitor and interpret meetings held at the Pentagon involving negotiations between the U.S. and other nations—both friendly and unfriendly.

"Since I haven't formally accepted their offer, mainly because I wanted to run it by the three of you first, they were reluctant to give many details. However, Vietnam came up twice during my interview. I concluded, since they were interviewing those fluent in Chinese, Russian, and Vietnamese, there must be something substantial brewing in Asia."

The waitress appears with our dinner. After she retreats, Chi asks, "Where would you have to go?"

"Not far. My office would be at the Pentagon, only thirty minutes from Herndon. Right in your backyard, Mom," Parker replies. "Why, I'd be close enough to bring my laundry home on the weekends and pick up a batch of fresh-baked cookies to take back with me."

Chi smiles.

Niàn remains unusually quiet the entire time. Looking thoughtful, he finally says, "America has been good to Chinese refugees who fled certain death because of their beliefs. We were afforded the opportunity to live free from tyranny and oppression, and having experienced freedom, I wouldn't want any other lifestyle. Not all people who live under dictatorships even know there is a different way of life. Sadly enough, things will never change for those trapped in those countries. That's just the way it is.

"Having said that, Parker, if your language skills will help American interests, and you're not in harm's way, if you decide to accept the position, you do so with our blessing." Niàn looks at Chi. She nods, then all three of them look at me.

Niàn's comments are most profound and strike a chord. I find it amazing that immigrants grasp the concepts of life, liberty, and happiness better than those born and raised in America. With that thought fresh in my mind, I begin: "I'm not sure how to respond. To be honest with you, Parker mentioning Vietnam gives me cause to worry. In October 1962, our country grappled with Russia during the Cuban missile crisis and were able to avoid a nuclear war.

Then, in August 1964, the U.S. entered the Vietnam war, and I'm not so sure Parker won't be drafted regardless of what path he chooses."

I hesitate mentioning other concerns for fear of spoiling the occasion, so I tread lightly. "As we all know, freedom isn't free! The price, especially in human life, is unimaginable. I've witnessed the horrors of war and am thankful that, as an interpreter, Parker wouldn't be exposed to actual combat. Not wanting him to be on the frontlines is perhaps selfish of me considering how many parents have lost and continue to lose their children defending our freedoms. However, the defense of freedom is an ongoing battle and one worth fighting. No one knows what the future holds." I take a deep breath and concede, "If Parker's skills promote the cause of freedom, I join Niàn and Chi in encouraging him to accept the offer. And turning to Parker, I say, "You can also count on my blessing if you decide to accept!"

The next day, before I leave for Charleston, over breakfast Parker advises the three of us, Niàn, Chi, and me, that he telephoned the office of the Secretary of Defense and accepted the position. Parker reminds me more and more that he's a chip off the old block. Not only in his looks and actions, but his love of a country that does not seek expansion and acquisition of territory like most conquerors but peaceful coexistence as its goal. In other words, a symbiotic relationship where everyone benefits.

Chapter Eight

Rhapsody in Blue

The beginning of the twentieth century ushered in the advent of a new way of life and 1903 was a banner year for inventions. The first Ford automobile was sold in July of 1903. Ironically, in December of the same year, the Wright brothers made their first successful flight with a powered airplane.

The rest is history. The widespread availability of trains, planes, ships, and automobiles was the wave of the future and the world kept getting smaller and smaller. The convenience of traveling from country to country made it much easier for enemy spies to move from place to place seeking to infiltrate and conquer other nations. America was not exempt. Disloyal, power-hungry government officials continuously searched for ways to usurp power. Some traitorous Americans even went so far as to aid and abet foreign and domestic terrorists in their quest to accomplish the destruction of the American way of life.

• • •

I'm forty-five years old when I retire from the military, and the only marketable skill I have is flying. On a hunch, I pay a visit to the local privately owned airfield and talk to the owner, Webster Farley, about starting an aviation school. At first, he seems uninterested. However, when I tell him about my service record, his interest is piqued.

Chewing on a matchstick, Farley rears back in a tattered leather desk chair with his feet propped on his desk and says, "So, you're a WW II ace, are ya?"

From his attitude, it's apparent he doesn't believe me. "That's right, Mr. Farley," I say. "I shot down so many enemy planes, my crew ran out of room to paint the kills on my fuselage."

Removing the matchstick from his mouth, Farley leans forward, eyes me up and down for a few moments, then roars with laughter. "Dammit, Parker! I like the cut of your jib. You've got spunk and guts. That's the attitude that won the war. You're hired!" After a pause, he adds, "And since this flying school is your idea, it's up to you to get it up and running. There's a shack at the far end of the field. It's yours to use any way you see fit. And I expect to see a profit by the end of the year!"

"Yes, sir!" I say with a flair. I stand and give him a smart salute.

We shake hands sealing the deal and he walks me to the door. "By the way, call me Webb."

And just like that, I've got myself the beginnings

of an aviation school.

• • •

Hank and I had kept in touch over the years and ironically, he, too, retired from the military the same year I did.

"Other than the Seabees, you're the only family I've ever had or even give a damn about," he says when I call. "I did some research and Charleston looks to me like a pretty good place to live, and besides, I'd be near you and the Zhēns. I kinda like being Uncle Hank."

Here we go! "Of course, you do," I chide. But before he can retort, I continue, "Your wanting to relocate to Charleston comes just in time!"

"How's that?" Hank asks.

"Upon my retirement from the military, I found myself at loose ends. Not wanting to give up flying, I had an idea, so I met with the proprietor of the local airfield and proposed we combine efforts and establish an aviation school. He was all for it and gave me the green light. He made it clear it was my baby. All he wants is a profit by the end of the year."

"Sounds like you got yourself a gig!" Hank replies.

"That I do. But I'll need help getting this gig off the ground, so to speak. If you're interested—"

"Hell yes, I'm interested! But, as you well

know, I don't know how to fly."

"Don't need to. I need a dependable ground person to run the office and keep books while I do the training." Holding my breath, I wait for an answer. It doesn't take long for Hank to respond.

"In that case, I'm your man!" Hank bellows, and I detect a smile in his voice. "I can be there by the end of the week."

• • •

When I take Hank to the airport and show him the small shack that was assigned to me to use as home base, he exclaims, "We can turn this dump into a respectable building in nothing flat. Think this Webb fellow would object to a makeover?"

"Don't think Webb would object in the least. Right now, it's an eyesore and I'm surprised it hasn't been condemned."

I immediately go to Webb's office and ask him about the remodel. He's all for it, as long as it doesn't cost him anything. When I assure him it won't, he readily agrees. In no time, Hank turns the shack into a first-class training center. He adds a classroom which can accommodate ten students. It's equipped with all the necessities including a blackboard. His addition more than doubles the size of the original structure.

At the conclusion of the remodel, Webb, Hank,

and I stand shoulder to shoulder admiring the building.

"Now all you need is a name," Webb comments.

"Already thought of that," says Hank. "Stay right where you are for just a minute." He then goes around the building and returns carrying what looks like some sort of sign under his arm. Positioning himself in front of us, he proudly displays it. Emblazoned in blue on a white background are the words "Rhapsody in Blue."

I don't remember doing it, but I must've mentioned to Hank at some time or another that the Gershwin composition, "Rhapsody in Blue," was one of my all-time favorites. I immediately like the concept. The word rhapsody certainly describes how I feel about flying and the prospect of teaching others to do so. Hopefully, our future students will be of the same mind. Blue is the color of the sky we hope for.

When no one immediately speaks, Hank apparently thinks we don't like the sign and mumbles, "Oh well, it was just an idea…" Tucking the sign back under his arm, he heads toward the rear of the building.

"Hold on there! Are you kidding!" I shout. "I love it! You captured the essence in three little words. Get your ladder. We're going to hang that baby above the door right now!"

"I'll help," Webb says. "Don't have any champagne but I have a bottle of beer we can bust over the bow and christen this ship."

• • •

When we're finally up and running, we generate much interest. I attribute the onslaught to the practice of theaters running newsreels between the featured motion pictures during the war. The newsreels depicted the action taking place across Europe and in the Pacific. The flying scenes must've been inspiring to movie goers because as soon as word spreads regarding our aviation school we were swamped with pilot wannabes.

Some of the students appear to be disappointed when they learn that the training doesn't all take place in the air. They are first required to complete and pass ground school courses. It's not as easy as learning to drive a car. Thanks to Hank's schoolroom addition, I'm able to keep up with the ground school instruction. I soon discover that one plane and one pilot isn't enough to keep up with the flying instruction, so I have a heart to heart with Webb.

"Right now, you're going great guns," Webb remarks. "The surge may just be a postwar passing fancy. I have a couple of Piper Cubs stored in one of the hangers. Let's refurbish them instead of investing in new planes. And I know some crack pilots who would volunteer to train just to log airtime. They can help with the actual flying instruction."

With the Pipers and two more pilots, the aviation school evolves into a roaring success. By midyear, Webb is making money hand over fist just renting his planes to aspiring pilots.

I couldn't help teasing him one afternoon when I took the daily flight schedule to his office. "Remember when you told me you wanted a profit by the end of the year? It's not even midyear and you've already made a significant profit. Have we lived up to your expectations?" I boldly ask.

"Hell yes!" he snorts. "You've more than lived up to your end of the bargain. You twerp! You're not old enough to butt heads with a seasoned back atcha professional like me, so don't get cocky."

I hang my head in feigned embarrassment and take a seat across from him.

Retrieving a slip of paper from his desktop, he hands it to me. "This call came in for you a few minutes ago."

I glance at the note and immediately recognize the phone number as that of the Zhēns. Since they've never phoned me at the airfield, fear instantly grips me. My first instinct is that something bad has happened to Parker. "It's from the Zhēns," I mutter. "Hope nothing's wrong."

"Only one way to find out," says Webb. "Stay here and use my phone. I'll step outside while you make the call."

My hands shake as I dial the long-distance operator and place the call.

• • •

I recognize Niàn's voice when the call is answered. "Hello," he says.

"Niàn, this is Steve. Is everything all right?"

"No, Steve. We've just been informed by the War Department that Parker and the other two interpreters have been kidnapped by the Viet Cong."

"The Viet Cong!" I shout. "What were the interpreters doing in Vietnam?"

"It appears they were sent there on a highly sensitive mission. Chi and I were told by the bearer of the bad news that the Vietnamese government arranged a secret meeting between their country, China, the U.S., and Russia in an attempt to negotiate an end to the war. Our War Department, apparently not trusting foreign interpreters, opted to send Parker and the other two to translate on behalf of the United States. That was a week ago."

"A week ago! What took so long for them to inform you that Parker had been kidnapped?" I blurt, unable to control my anger and conceal my disgust.

"That was my question," Niàn says. "However, the official that paid us the visit told us he was not privy to any other information, only that the department was working on a plan to get Parker and the other two interpreters released."

"That's less than comforting!" I snort and quickly add, "I still have a few connections with the military. I'll see what I can find out and get back to you." I realize Niàn and Chi must be terrified for Parker's safety, so I say, "Tell Chi to try not to worry. I *will* get Parker back alive! I promise you that! And it won't be by negotiation!"

• • •

Being ex-military, I try to keep informed of the world events involving conflicts and know some of the major causes triggering the Vietnam War were the spread of communism during the Cold War, American containment, and European influence. It's a known fact that the Viet Cong, is a part of the communist guerilla movement and is supplied with arms, missiles, and fuel by the Russians.

When panic and confusion sink in, my brain is on information overload and I, too, fear for the safety of Parker as well as the other two interpreters. I hang up the phone and rush to the office door. When I jerk it open, I collide with Webb who is just entering from the opposite side. "Whoa, partner. What's the hurry?" he asks.

"Viet Cong kidnapped Parker…" is all I can mutter as I rush down the corridor toward the exit. Webb is right behind me. We reach the school in short order, and as we enter, I shout for Hank.

Hank immediately appears from the empty classroom holding a broom. Dropping the broom, he grips me by the shoulders stopping me midstride. "What's goin' on, Steve?" he demands with concern written on his face.

"Just talked to Niàn. He told me they had just been informed that the Viet Cong had kidnapped Parker and the other two interpreters …" Gasping for air, I pause and take a deep breath.

"Parker is in Vietnam?" Hank asks in a stunned voice.

"Yes! I've got to get over there…" I stammer as I pace the floor.

"Okay, I'm with you but slow down! We need to formulate a plan and not just go off half-cocked," Hank says and points to one of the chairs in the classroom. "Take a seat and let's think this thing through—"

"I agree!" Webb says only steps behind me. "You definitely need a plan and anything I have that you can use, consider it yours. I'll get some help running the school while the two of you are on the rescue mission."

I nod, finally slowing down long enough to absorb the gravity of the situation and the need to be objective and dispassionate.

Hank slips into the seat next to me. "The first hurdle to overcome is finding out where they're being held. The War Department may give that information to you since you're Parker's biological father. If not, there's more than one way to skin a cat. Next, we need to figure out how to get into Vietnam."

"I can help with that," says Webb, and removes the ever-present matchstick from his mouth. "Following the end of World War II, I researched various locations across the globe that people might want to visit and calculated the mileage to come up with possible airfares. It seems China has always been a favorite place for tourists, so I did in-depth research on flying times from here to the major cities in China. For example, it's about eighteen hours flying time from Charleston to Shanghai."

Hank and I both stare at Webb in astonishment. Unabashed by our expressions, Webb continues,

"With the Vietnam war raging, our government has restricted U.S. citizens' travel to China. If you have the resources, and you do," Webb says pointing to himself, "it can be done. If Shanghai is the jump-off place, getting to Shanghai will be the easy part, and I can arrange that. Getting to wherever it's determined they're being held beyond Shanghai will be the hard part."

Hank and I, still overwhelmed by Webb's wealth of information, sit in stunned silence when he goes to the blackboard and draws a crude map of the China-Vietnam boarder, tracing the route from Shanghai to Hanoi with a piece of chalk. "Using two major cities in Vietnam and China, as the crow flies, Shanghai to Hanoi is approximately 1200 miles. All commercial flights have been rerouted or suspended over that area because of the war. When you get to Shanghai, if you could commandeer a small aircraft the trip into Vietnam would take four to five hours. And depending on the fuel capacity of the plane, you might have to find someplace to refuel enroute, that is if you don't get shot down before you run out of fuel. The bottom line is that at some point, you may have to travel a long arduous distance on foot across hostile territory—mostly jungle."

Still flabbergasted by Webb's knowledge of the

Asian continent, I say, "I'm impressed! Any idea where the hostages might be held?"

"My first guess would be Hanoi, that's why I used it in my example. But I'm just the travel agent, so you're on your own there!" Webb retorts as he reinserts the matchstick and takes a seat.

• • •

After I met with Hank and Webb, I contact the War Department at the Pentagon. I'm not surprised to get the runaround.

The cheery receptionist recites what sounds like a canned response for people in my situation. "We're sorry, Mr. Parker. It's against policy to divulge any information regarding captives. However, I can assure you we're on top of it and in the process of engaging in negotiations to obtain the release of all the American prisoners—"

Disappointed and disgusted, I hang up before she can complete her spiel. When I tell Hank about the response I received from the War Department, he reassures me he still has contacts and that his people would get the information for us. And true to his word, before we leave for Shanghai, Hank finds out from a reliable source that Parker and the other two interpreters are being held at one of the Viet Cong rebels' makeshift prison facilities on the outskirts of Hanoi.

"It might be one of the bombed-out temples," Hank reports. "I'm told that part of the red pagoda-style roof remains intact and could be used as a source of identification. My source also told me that the theory is when the recent attempt to negotiate an end to the war fell through, the three Americans who were sent to interpret the summit were taken prisoner and are being held hostage by the rebels as leverage. So far, no ransom or other concession has been demanded, so no one knows for sure what the rebels have in mind." After a pause, Hank continues. "I hate to be the one to say this out loud, but when I was in the service, our country never gave in to blackmail demands in order to free hostages."

Once again fear wraps its icy fingers around my heart. "I know," I say. "I'm thinking that since the interpreters are civilian and not military, that might make a difference in obtaining their release."

"Not with the kind of people we're dealing with," Hank responds. "All's fair in love and war is how they think and operate. Never mind the humanitarian aspect of combat. They'll do whatever, and I mean whatever, it takes to get the job done!"

"Another concern I have is that various drugs and hypnosis are now being used by the Asians to brainwash prisoners of war. After weeks of brainwashing, I've been told the victims are sent home programmed to report back to their captors any significant information they uncover. The hypnosis process is so sophisticated and clandestine, even the victims are unaware they've been programmed. The Cong probably thought they hit the jackpot when they kidnapped Chinese, Vietnamese, and Russian-speaking interpreters in one fell swoop to use as spies." Massaging my temples, I add, "Sounds to me like an updated version of the Trojan Horse subversion tactic. By the way, did your source indicate how well guarded the prison facility is?"

"No," says Hank, "but if they only have the three prisoners, civilians at that, I'm assuming not too many guards will be posted on duty at any one time. The interpreters are noncombatants and are probably not thought to pose much of a threat. Manpower can best be used on the battlefield, not guarding three civilian captives."

• • •

Based on that assumption, Hank and I do our homework. We research Hanoi in the most recent edition of the World Book Encyclopedia as well as the surrounding areas. The photographs are outdated but one depicts a temple with a red pagoda-style roof. It's situated on the outskirts of Hanoi.

"Think that may be our target?" I ask as we study the photo.

"Umm, unless another temple was constructed after the photo was printed in the WBE which was copyrighted in…" Hank pauses and turns to the front of the book, "1950. That's fairly current," he muses.

"Right you are. And like Christian churches," I reply. "The temples are spaced so as not to compete with each other."

Hank closes the encyclopedia. "Since this is the only lead we have," he exclaims, "let's go for it. Better than sitting here doing nothing."

Hank's determination is contagious, and optimism is building. We know that time is not on our side, so we immediately begin to prepare for the tedious and dangerous journey that awaits us.

Chapter Nine

Far Away Places

Although American travel to China is restricted during the Vietnam war, Hank and I, with Webb's help, are able to fly to Shanghai masquerading as Chinese-Americans returning home to China. When we arrive, the airport in Shanghai is in utter chaos, so when we deplane, we're able to blend into the crowded terminal without being questioned.

We press our way through the congestion and once we're out on the street, the sights, scents, and sounds of the city transport me back to 1942. Memories of Su Lin flood my mind and I must force myself not to get lost in the melancholy of the past. *If I survive this mission, I'll make it a point to find a way to revisit Wai Sang,* I promise myself.

"Hey, Steve, come on," Hank interrupts my reverie. "I've got a taxi."

Shouldering my seabag, I hurry to the curb where Hank has a taxi waiting. I look up and down the street before entering the cab. China is the most populated country in the world, and they all seem to be congregated on this one street. Fortunately, our driver is a seasoned veteran and bullies his way into the stream of traffic. There are a lot of near misses as those in our path scramble for safety. Our driver deftly maneuvers his way through traffic and miraculously deposits us safely at our hotel.

When we enter the lobby of the hotel, I remark, "Things sure have changed over the last twenty years—or perhaps I just didn't notice the state of things when I was here."

"That's because you were pretty much restricted to the village of Wai Sang which does not reflect China as a whole, my friend. You were insulated from the real thing," Hank says. "When I was with the construction crew, I lived in this very hotel for over a year and got to be fairly well acquainted with the geography, the people, and the colloquialisms."

When we finally arrive at our room, I drop my seabag onto the floor and plop down on my bed. I'm so travel-weary, my head is spinning. "Think I'll take a nap before dinner." I curl up on the lumpy bed and am soon sound asleep. My dreams are haunted with images of Su Lin, I can even smell the fragrance of her hair. *"I wait for you in bonsai garden,"* I hear her say. *"You must save our boy. I help you."*

"Steve, Steve, wake up," a voice penetrates my dreams. I don't want to wake up and turn over, hoping the intruder will go away. "Oh, no you don't," the voice persists. "We're on a mission! Now get your butt outta bed!"

Struggling to a sitting position, I scratch my head as I remember the dream. "Hank, Su Lin appeared to me in a dream. She said she'd help us find Parker."

"Sure, sure!" Hank replies sarcastically.

I'm disappointed at Hank's cavalier attitude. Even if he doesn't believe, I do. I know Su Lin visited me and will help us save Parker.

• • •

After we freshen up, we go to one of Hank's old haunts for dinner. Although the atmosphere isn't inspiring, the food is great. Some of the staff, even after all these years, recognize Hank and greet him with smiles, bows, and handshakes.

"Hank-son," one elderly waiter says. "We miss you. Where you go?"

"Home to America," Hank replies.

"What you do back in Shanghai?"

"Uh, giving my friend here," Hank points to me, "a tour of your city."

"I see. Much changed since you here. But we have same menu. Hope you *rike* dinner."

Hank remarks, "I'm sure we will." When Hank orders, I follow suit, ordering the same since I don't read Chinese. And to my delight, the dinner is excellent as promised. I even learn the technique of using chopsticks with Hank's help.

• • •

Back in our room after dinner, we review our list of the must-haves we need to take into Vietnam. Our first order of business is to acquire weapons. Not only does Hank know the geography, people, and colloquialisms, he also has a battery of Chinese contacts he established while working construction here before the start of WW II.

Once our list is compiled, we don't waste time and venture out into the night seeking Hank's Chinese contacts. The streets are lined with a variety of shops, and in short order, I find the innocent-looking items displayed for sale are a front for more sinister goods sold under the table. We're soon equipped with binoculars, camouflage clothing, hand grenades, AK-47 automatic rifles, machetes, lots of bug repellant, and a snakebite kit. Malarial mosquitoes, leeches, ticks, fire ants and poisonous snakes prowl the jungle, not to mention the hazardous Viet Cong booby traps scattered throughout the terrain.

• • •

Back in our room we take stock of our gear. With a little ingenuity we manage to pack all our supplies into our Navy seabags. When we finish, Hank remarks, "Looks like we're ready for the journey, especially if we encounter opposition, and I'm not referring just to the human variety. Now all we need is transportation."

That thought had been niggling at my brain for some time. Trekking some 1200 miles through a hostile jungle toting a heavy seabag and an AK-47 has little appeal. "Any suggestions?"

"Maybe," Hank replies. "An old acquaintance of mine, Píng Lee, has or had a helicopter. He used to fly supplies to the construction site from the airport. If he's still around, and willing to do it, he can fly us inland and then follow the Red River to within a hundred miles of Hanoi. It would be too dangerous for him to go further. Then, with any luck at all, we can 'requisition' a boat to take us upriver the rest of the way."

"Looks good on paper," I say. "How do we proceed from here?"

"It's been my experience that the Chinese don't move around much. Although its been a while, I still remember how to get to Píng's place. Tomorrow morning we'll locate Píng and play it by ear. If Píng is unwilling to fly us in, maybe he knows someone who will. In the meantime, let's get some shuteye. We may not have a chance to get much after we start our hike."

• • •

Having a sense of accomplishment thus far, I sleep fairly well. The next morning, we're up as the sun is just rising. Although apprehensive, I'm excited to finally get started on our quest to find the kidnapped interpreters and especially Parker. The streets are quiet in contrast to the hubbub we encountered the night before.

After checking out of the hotel, we hail a taxi and load our seabags into the trunk. Since we don't have a physical address, Hank guides the driver to a small hut on the outskirts of Shanghai. As we approach the dwelling, I see a helicopter setting on a pad not far from the hut. From my vantage point, the chopper looks to be in good condition—at least there are no visible bullet holes in the fuselage.

We exit the cab but before I can pay the driver, a middle-aged Chinese man emerges from the hut and greets us. "Nǐhǎo," the man says as he approaches. Apparently recognizing Hank, he adds, "Hank-son, welcome to my humble jiā."

"Hello, Píng," Hank says returning the greeting, and the two old friends engage in a back-slapping hug. When Hank disengages, he points to me, and says, "This is my long-time friend Steve Parker."

"Happy to meet Hank-son's friend," Píng says and bows.

I bow back.

"I make tea, you join me?" and without waiting for a reply, Píng turns back towards the hut and motions for us to follow.

Once inside, the three of us sit cross-legged on straw mats on the floor and Píng pours tea into a hodgepodge assortment of cups. When I start to pick up my cup, Hank ever so slightly shakes his head. I get the message and wait. Píng finishes the service, returns the teapot to the stove, and joins us. We then partake in what appears to be a religious ritual before drinking the pungent tea. After taking a few sips, Píng asks, "What bring you here?"

Hank nods in my direction, "Steve's son has been taken prisoner by the Viet Cong."

"Ha, I see," Píng remarks. "How may I help?" he asks as he retrieves the pot and pours another round.

"We need a ride," Hank says and gestures towards the location where the helicopter sits. "As close as you can get us to Hanoi."

"Oh, not go Hanoi!" Píng blurts. "Much danger."

"We know, but if you can get us to the Red River and within a hundred miles of Hanoi, we can manage from there."

Píng shrinks back and furrows his brow. I fear he's going to refuse our request.

"I can do," Píng remarks as the hesitation or indecision disappears. "I repay Hank-son for much kindness. Buddha say Chinese must always repay kindness."

Hank bows.

Píng bows back. "How soon?" he asks.

"Today?" Hank queries placing the decision squarely on Píng.

"I can do," Píng replies without further hesitation. "I dream you ask this, and dream say I do for you. Dream say we wait for sundown. Make hard for Cong to see chopper in sky."

Su Lin?

• • •

We spend the rest of the morning preparing for departure. Píng has several gas-filled containers on hand, and we help him top off the helicopter's fuel tank. When he fires it up, I watch him take the pilot's seat and test the various gauges. Apparently satisfied all systems are go, he hops down from the cockpit.

"Ready to load," he says.

It suddenly occurs to me that Píng will have to refuel for the return trip. "Píng, how will you get back here?"

"I fly back," he replies and narrows his eyes giving me a strange look.

"No, I know that but where will you get fuel for the return trip?"

"Ah! Many Vietnamese friendly. I make pit

stop on way back."

I pull my wallet from my pants pocket. "How much money will you—"

"No! No money!" Píng says and waves his hands rejecting the offer. "Vietnamese found with U.S. dollars die bad death."

"How can I repay you then?" I ask.

"No repay. Do this for Hank-son," Píng says with a broad smile.

Hank and I carry our seabags loaded with supplies to the open hatch. Hank hoists himself aboard and I hand the seabags and AK-47 rifles up to him. He stores them making sure the load is evenly distributed in the cargo area of the chopper. Píng stands by watching. When we're finished, Hank jumps down and looks at his watch.

"We have a few hours before sunset," Hank says. "We should try to get some sleep."

"Ah," Píng replies. "I have sleep mats. Come, we go to hut."

• • •

Two hours later, I'm awakened by the clattering of what sounds like someone cooking. When I sit up and look around, Hank says, "Just in time! Píng has prepared a late lunch. By the time we finish, it'll be time to go."

Rubbing my eyes, I ask, "What's on the menu

for the last supper?"

"Special Chinese dish and I'm not sure what's in it. However, it smells pretty darn good. Other than the MREs we brought with us; this may well be our so-called last supper—for a while anyway."

Once again, we sit on the straw mats and use chopsticks to eat the meal. Chewing on a thick slice of bread, Hank remarks, "You fly boys had it pretty good during the war, hot meals three times a day, nice warm bunks to curl up on and oh, yes, showers. Us grunts not so much. Most of the time we fended for ourselves."

I can't argue with Hank's perception. Aboard ship, we did have it pretty good compared to the other branches of service. Knowing the daunting trip that lies before us, I don't reflect on those easy years for fear I'll falter. Thank God Hank's spearheading this gig. With his service time in the field, he's a seasoned veteran with lots of experience. Me? I'm just a pampered jet jockey.

Píng's special dish is so tasty, I eat two servings. When I offer to help with the cleanup, Píng says, "No time. We go now. No wait, sun soon gone."

• • •

Píng's liftoff is flawless, and I relax a little. However, my comfort zone is soon shattered when the jungle comes into view. From our altitude we can see the expanse of jungle foliage that awaits us, and it looks unforgiving. I cringe when I think I'll soon be in the midst of all that unfamiliar hostile terrain. About an hour into our flight, I see a river snaking its way through the thick jungle.

"There it is," Hank shouts over the roar of the engine and the flap-flap of the propellers. "That's the Red River, our roadmap."

"That was quick," I comment.

"Take it easy, partner. We still have a way to go before we land," says Hank. "Píng will follow the river for another two hours to get us further into Vietnam territory. After that…"

I'm riding in the cargo area and am already anxious about our mission. Hank's "after that" comment only adds to my fear, and when I view the terrain we'll ultimately be going through, I begin to wonder if this was such a great idea after all. No sooner than that worrisome thought penetrates my brain than a vision of Parker appears in my head.

Su Lin?

• • •

Sometime later into the flight, my thoughts are interrupted when I hear Píng say, "This is far as I go. I land there," and he points to a clearing close to the river. "I think Hanoi not too far, maybe hundred miles." Píng says.

A hundred miles through hostile jungle! I cringe at the thought of leaving the comfort and security of the chopper.

Once we're on the ground, we waste no time unloading. When we finish, Hank shouts, "Píng, your service has been above and beyond expectations. Thank you, my friend. Hopefully, we'll see you on our return trip. You take care."

"I be okay, *you* take care," Píng responds. Returning to the cockpit, Píng gives us a farewell wave and revving the engine, he starts his ascent. Hank and I hunker down and place our arms over our heads to shield us from the downdraft. When Píng is airborne, we stand and watch the chopper fade into the evening sky. As soon as it's out of sight, the ominous sounds of the jungle invade the stillness. Although it's hot and humid, I'm seized with chills and my skin crawls just thinking of the vermin that awaits us beyond the clearing.

• • •

Hank breaks the spell when he begins rustling around in one of the seabags. Finding a tube of bug repellant, he squeezes a gob onto his palm. Then, handing me the tube, says, "Here, put a generous amount of this on *all* exposed skin."

Once we're sufficiently greased up, Hank utters, "Hopefully, we can find an abandoned boat fairly soon." He then hoists one of the seabags onto a shoulder and slings an AK-47 across his chest. "Let's go, partner. We're burnin' twilight." Hoisting my gear, I fall in directly behind him.

• • •

Not accustomed to traveling with boots on the ground, I'm clumsy and readjust my load periodically to keep from stumbling. The heat and humidity are overwhelming. Sweat laden with bug repellant drips into my eyes, causing them to sting and water. I swipe at them with my shirt sleeves which only makes the stinging worse. Hank appears to be adapting to the adverse conditions much better than yours truly.

We travel along the riverbank for a few miles before Hank holds up his hand. I peer past him and see a boat tethered to a wooden dock. No one is in sight.

"Manna from heaven," Hank whispers.

Keeping low, we creep to the dock. I constantly look behind us, expecting to be jumped by the boatowner. No one appears, so we load our gear into the boat. Hank takes the helm while I untie the rope, push away from the dock, and jump aboard. We use the oars and row downriver a few hundred yards before starting the motor. Much to my surprise, the engine starts on the first try and we're off to the races.

Mirroring my thoughts, Hank utters, "That was just too easy!"

"You think it's a trap of some sort?" I ask.

"Don't know but so far so good. I think the owner is just too complacent and has let his guard down," Hank says. "Whatever the circumstance, his loss is our gain."

Darkness is closing in and we stay close to the riverbank where we're partially hidden by the jungle overgrowth. Hank is doing the navigating and I have my weapon ready, watching for hostiles along the shore. Suddenly, a large black snake drops from one of the trees into our boat. Without thinking twice, I flip the snake overboard with the barrel of my AK-47 and watch it slither away in the opposite direction. I shudder thinking of the encounter. Snakes are not my thing!

"You should've seen the look on your face!" Hank drawls, grinning at me.

"Yeah. And if you think that's funny, you should see what I did in my shorts," I retort.

Hank cringes. "Don't sit close to me!"

• • •

We travel the river until the boat runs out of fuel and then row ashore. We're now faced with another dilemma. It's now pitch dark.

"Steve, we have a choice. We can spend the night on the boat taking turns on watch or we can chance going through the jungle in the dark. Your call."

The snake encounter is still fresh in my mind, and I certainly don't want to encounter any more jungle critters after dark. "Uh, let's stay on the boat."

"Good choice! Things that live out there can usually see in the dark—we can't."

I volunteer to take the first watch. Our surroundings are foreign and hostile, and I don't think I could've slept anyway. The sounds from the jungle intensify after dark. The temperature is more tolerable even though it's still extremely humid. The noises surrounding me reminds me of my first visit to a zoo and keeps me awake and vigilant. After a few hours, Hank and I switch places. By this time, I'm so exhausted, I'm able to ignore the jungle rumble and snooze for a while. The night passes without incident. At first light, we're ready. We abandon the boat and head into the jungle.

• • •

Hank estimates we're within earshot and eyeshot of our target. We're careful not to be discovered. The foliage closes in behind us. We do not talk, and if I lose sight of Hank, I fear I'd be lost forever in this godforsaken hellhole. Hank moves slowly and often signals for me to stop as he uses the machete to carefully probe the path in front of us testing for booby traps and anything else that might be a hazard.

About an hour into our journey, Hank holds up a hand. He puts a finger to his lips. I hear voices coming from the direction in which we're traveling. Hank steps back and pulls me aside. We hunker down in the dense jungle foliage beside the path. As we crouch in our hide, we're instantly covered with insects and fire ants. The bug repellant dissuades the insects; however, the ants are relentless. There are millions of them, and I wonder how in the hell they found us so fast. They swarm over our boots. Hank looks at me and shakes his head. He knows I'm fighting the urge to swat the ants away.

The voices come closer. I scrunch lower and hold my breath. I don't understand the conversation, but the chatter is laced with occasional laughter, and it sounds like two or three of what must be Viet Cong soldiers headed in our direction. If they're being so noisy and even laughing, they obviously haven't detected or even suspected our presence.

We're crouching close to the path, and from our vantage point, we're able to catch a glimpse of their boots as they pass. As soon as the voices fade into the distance, I'm eager to get rid of the ants, and make a move to do so. Hank puts a restraining hand on my shoulder and once again shakes his head. A few moments later, another trio of soldiers pass.

· · ·

When Hank finally determines it's safe to break cover, we go on. They've beaten a path and it's easier to travel without having to probe for booby traps every step. We make good time and soon, just like night turns into day, the jungle is behind us and we're at the edge of a clearing. Taking stock of our position, we spot a temple in the distance. We observe a group of five uniformed soldiers with weapons huddled together.

"That temple looks like the one we saw in the encyclopedia," I whisper. "It even has a red pagoda roof."

Since the guards are so close to the temple, we conclude the soldiers we observed must be from the prison.

"I think we've found where the captives are being held," Hank whispers as he scans the area with the binoculars.

My heart begins to race when I realize we may be within striking distance of the rescue mission. If it fails, Hank and I may be joining Parker and the other two interpreters behind bars. That is, if we're lucky enough to still be alive. I'm willing to trade my life for Parker's and that's my driving force.

Chapter Ten

Accentuate the Positive

Although the trek through the jungle was rough going, at least the dense foliage provided some camouflage. As I view the distance to the temple from where we're standing, I notice there's very little cover between here and there. It appears to me to be a suicide mission if we attempt to cross the open space in broad daylight. I glance at Hank. His focus is on scraping mud from the soles of his boots with his bayonet and he doesn't appear to be the least bit concerned about our upcoming exposure.

"What's our next move?" I whisper.

Hank straightens and slices a large leaf from the jungle foliage. He then wipes the mud from his bayonet with the leaf and stores the bayonet in the sheath attached to his duty belt. Raising the binoculars to his eyes, he scans the terrain, and comments, "If my sources were correct, I'm inclined to believe this most likely is the prison where Parker and the others are being held. And the only way to find out is to get inside." He then adds, "After dark, we'll advance and take a closer look. In the meantime, we'll stay here out of sight and use the binoculars to determine the guards' routine and when they rotate. That'll give us an advantage."

I fight the urge to storm the castle with guns blazing and rescue the captives. But discretion is the better part of valor, so I tamp down my anxiety. Hank hasn't been wrong yet and I have the utmost faith in his decisions and marvel at his patience.

Resigning myself to spending another few hours in the dreadful jungle, I volunteer to take the first watch. Hank moves back into the cover of the foliage and sits. Pulling up his knees, he folds his arms across them, and rests his forehead on his arms. I take up a position where I can see what appears to be the temple entrance. An hour or so into my watch, I notice movement and scan the terrain with the binoculars. I don't see anything and conclude the movement must've been an animal, as nothing of interest comes into view.

A few minutes later, five soldiers march up to the temple. They enter and soon, what looks like a different group of five soldiers, exit.

"Hank," I whisper, "are you awake?"

Hank is immediately alert, "What's up?"

I hand him the binoculars, "Looks like the changing of the guard," I say.

"How many?" he whispers as he takes the binoculars and scans the area for himself.

"Five went in, and what looked like five different ones came out," I respond.

"That's encouraging. If that's all the guards they have, I think we can handle 'em," Hank muses while still scanning the terrain. Then looking at the sky, he says, "Still have a couple of hours before it's dark enough to explore. My turn to take the watch—you rest."

Although I'm excited at the thought that we may be close to finding the kidnapped Americans, I allow fatigue to have its way. I retreat into the foliage and sit in the same manner as did Hank. Thankfully, the fire ants stayed behind. However, we still have the flying insects to contend with, so I smear another layer of bug repellant on my exposed skin. The minute I relax, I fall into a fitful slumber. When Hank rouses me, it's pitch dark, and it takes me a minute or two to orient to my surroundings. An eerie feeling grips me as total darkness presses in around us.

"Time to go," Hank says.

The rush of advancing on the target causes me to experience the same emotions I had during the war before engaging in a combat mission. Adrenalin surges through my veins and all my senses are on high alert. "I'm ready." I shoulder my seabag. Hank hangs the binoculars around his neck and takes the lead. We both carry our AK-47s at the ready should we encounter opposition.

The city of Hanoi is in full blackout and the only illumination we have comes from the moon that disappears from time to time behind the clouds. Hank must've planned our route during his watch. I'm behind him when he breaks cover and creeps along, sidestepping obstacles. Keeping a low profile, I mimic his every move. After a few agonizing minutes the silhouette of the temple comes into view, and we advance to within several feet of the entrance. My instinct tells me this indeed is where Parker and the others are being held. My heart begins to race.

Hank holds up a hand signaling me to stop. We stand and listen for a few moments. The only sounds come from the jungle.

"That's odd," Hank whispers. "The guards can't all be asleep, that would mean a date with the firing squad."

Hank no sooner gets the words out than we're attacked by a single guard who comes at us from behind. I take a blow to the small of my back. It feels like I've been hit with the butt of a rifle. Although the blow is buffered by my seabag, it nonetheless knocks me to my knees. As I struggle to rise, Hank pulls his bayonet from his belt. The attacker turns from me and lunges at Hank. Hank's bayonet impales him. He grunts and drops to the ground.

Hank, wiping the blood from the bayonet onto the guard's uniform, returns it to its sheath. We drag the dead guard into the brush alongside the building and hurry into the interior of the temple.

In a hushed tone, Hank says, "It appears we've not been detected. Our ambusher may have been a lone wolf looking for a medal. The Cong wouldn't let their guard down and just let us causally walk in if they suspected anything was amiss—unless their arrogance and boredom clouded their better judgment."

Glancing over my shoulder, I peer into the darkness as I follow Hank into the temple wondering how he can be so composed. Later he would say his brazen was nothing more than a front and a coping mechanism.

Inside, the only light provided is by candles placed in wall sconces along a wide corridor. It appears the prisoners' cells are at the far end of the temple. Hank motions for me to proceed down the left side of the corridor while he proceeds down the right.

The candles flicker in the breeze that flows through the corridor and shadows dance on the walls and ceiling. Every shadow and every sound, no matter how slight, seems to be magnified.

Hank and I cautiously proceed toward the rear of the temple. We both stop dead in our tracks when we hear voices coming from somewhere in front of us. Hank puts a finger to his lips and looks around searching for a place to hide.

I see some stone benches in the shadows along the wall a few feet ahead of us. Hank gestures for me to follow him. We creep to the benches, keeping our weapons at the ready. We crouch in separate spaces between the benches and ease our seabags beneath them. We're wearing dark clothing and I hope we won't be seen. I hold my breath as two soldiers come into view headed toward us. They're chatting noisily and appear to be absorbed in conversation. Without so much as a glance in our direction, they strut past. Once they're far enough away, I breathe a sigh of relief.

Moments later, Hank breaks cover and duckwalks to where I'm crouching. He points to a chamber on the right. Pulling a hand grenade from his crossbody belt, he clutches it in his right hand and motions for me to stay close behind him. Pressing his back against the stone wall, he sidesteps to the chamber's opening.

As a Navy pilot, I've been involved in numerous air battles but never hand-to-hand combat. Other than at bootcamp, this is all new, and I have a knot in the pit of my stomach and suddenly my mouth is bone dry. Not knowing what to expect, I grow tense. As quick as apprehension seizes me, it's replaced by resolve and a feeling of calm when I remember why I'm here—to rescue Parker.

Su Lin?

Hank's a few paces in front of me, and he turns and signals for me to catch up. We're now very close to the chamber opening where voices are coming from. Hank stops us just before we get to an open doorway. Abruptly giving me the signal to halt, with his back still pressed against the wall, he advances to the opening and takes a quick peek into the room. Everything seems to be happening in slow motion which I know is not the case. I tense up expecting to now be confronted by the source of the voices. However, they apparently don't notice Hank's recon because the tone of their conversation doesn't change.

Still with his back against the wall outside the doorway Hank motions for me to get down. When I see him put the grenade to his mouth and remove the pin with his teeth, I squat and cover my head with my arms. Hank rolls the grenade into the room and joins me. Seconds later the silence is shattered by the explosion.

"C'mon, Steve!" Hank shouts, pulling on my arm.

My ears ring from the explosion, and as we race toward the rear of the temple, I shout Parker's name. Someone shouts back. It's Parker.

"Hank, that's Parker!" I blurt suddenly filled with renewed energy. Before we get much farther into the temple, we come under fire from behind and we immediately hit the floor. The slugs ping above our heads and randomly scatter as they ricochet off the marble ceiling and walls along the dimly lit corridor.

We return fire and a few moments into the fray, Hank shouts over the din, "You go find the boys! I'll hold off the enemy"

"But—" I begin.

"GO!" Hank demands.

I stay low, glancing at Hank. I watch him crawl to the wall and overturn one of the stone benches taking up a position behind it.

Terrified, I find my feet and run down the corridor. I call again, "Parker!" When he responds, "Dad!" I zero in on his probable location and soon locate the prison cells. Although the area is dimly lit, I can see several prisoners gathered at the front of the cell.

"Parker," I cry and clasp his hands through the

bars. After a brief reunion, I ask as I look around, "Where's the keys?"

"The guards keep them!"

We've no time to waste. "Stand back," I order and when the captives are far enough away from the cell door, I place a single shot into the lock with my sidearm. Once the door is breached, Parker and two other captives rush out. I assume the other two are the interpreters who were kidnapped along with Parker. Other prisoners are clamoring to be released so I go down the line unlocking the cells with carefully placed shots.

Leave No American Behind! has always been America's motto, and with Hank's help, I intend not to.

Soon, all the captives are out of their cells, and I'm standing amid ten grateful freed Americans. Seven identify themselves as Marines.

I motion for them to line up and follow in single file behind me. Before we start to advance, Parker steps up. "Dad, there's another prisoner. He's Vietnamese but he helped us. If we leave him, he'll be considered a traitor and the Cong will torture and kill him."

"Where is he?" I ask.

"They keep him separated from the Americans," Parker replies and points to a wooden door at the rear of the prison area.

I hand my AK-47 to one of the Marines. "You cover until I get back." The Marine nods and accepts the rifle. Then, in military fashion, he checks the chamber. *Good man! It's wise to make sure you have ammunition if you're headed into a gunfight.*

I say to the others, "All of you stay here." I hurry toward the rear of the cell block. "Stand back!" I shout and a moment later I blast the lock on the wooden door. I kick the door open. A thin oriental male kneels on the straw-covered floor. I rush to his side and pull him to his feet. "You speak English?" I ask. He nods. "Okay then, c'mon, we're leaving this hellhole!"

When he appears reluctant to follow me, I pull him along and we join the other freed prisoners. We form a line, and retracing my steps back down the corridor, we head into the sound of a ferocious gun battle.

"Hank!" I shout. "We're coming up behind you." By the time we hookup with Hank, the battle appears to be over. In the dim light we can see the corridor before us is strewn with bodies. Hank is down on one knee behind a stone bench, sporadically firing at anything and everything that moves in front of him.

Glancing over his shoulder, and spotting the freed prisoners, blurts, "Looks like you hit the jackpot! We need to get moving. This scrimmage most likely has alerted everyone within earshot."

We make our way to the exit, and as we pass dead bodies strewn along the corridor Hank orders our group to pick up the weapons and whatever ammo they can find. Some even sling two rifles over their shoulder in case we encounter another contingent of Viet Cong.

When we're outside of the temple, Parker stops us. "Wait, Dad," he says, "we were transported here from Hanoi in the back of an open truck. We passed an airfield enroute. It's not far from here—"

"Which way?" Hank interrupts.

Parker takes a moment to orient himself, then points west. "That direction," he says.

· · ·

It's still dark when we reenter the jungle on the other side of the temple. I'm concerned about the booby traps and mention it to Hank. "How can we avoid booby traps in the dark?" I ask.

Hank replies, "With all the activity around the temple, and being this close to the city, I'm thinking this side of the jungle hasn't been booby trapped. Besides, there must be a base somewhere close where the off-duty personnel hang out. And that being the case, we don't have time to weigh the odds. Our choices are taking a chance that this part of the jungle hasn't been booby trapped or waiting until daylight to proceed. If we wait, we'll most likely have to engage in another gun battle with possibly adverse results." After a pause, Hank asks, "What do you think we should do?"

"Looking around at the diminished state of the prisoners," I reply, "I don't think we'd have a chance in hell of even winning a dog fight without substantial cover. Unseen we stand a chance. Spotted, we better start digging our graves."

"Let's go!" Hank orders as he and two of the Marines take the point, and the rest of us fall in behind. Using his compass, Hank leads us in the direction Parker indicated.

"Be prepared," Hank cautions. "Just because we haven't been attacked yet doesn't mean they aren't planning a surprise. Don't think they know we have a pilot with us so they may discount the possibility that we're headed for the airfield and end up conducting the search in the wrong direction."

Most of the prisoners are weak so we travel slowly. Approximately an hour into our march, I hear a plane overhead. It's flying low, probably preparing to land. *We must be getting close to the airfield.* I'm astounded that we haven't encountered any opposition, and when Hank suddenly holds up a hand signaling for us to halt, my heart begins to thump. As we gather in a tight group around him, he pulls some tall foliage aside, allowing us to see what's before us.

"We've made it to the airfield," Hank whispers. We peer through the opening and watch the plane taxi to a Quonset hut terminal. "The distance from here to the aircraft parked on the tarmac is wide open space and could prove to be disastrous." Hank looks at me, Hank says, "You're the jet jockey. Take your pick of planes and we'll commandeer it!"

Hank's enthusiasm is contagious, and my misgivings quickly dissipate.

"We need a transport large enough to carry twelve passengers and a pilot," I reply as I zero in on a jet about the size of a U.S. C-12 Huron military transport. It looks exactly like what we need, and to boot, a tanker is just pulling away meaning it just finished refueling the plane. I point to the jet and say, "That's the one I'd pick!"

"Good choice. It was owned by a little ol' lady from Pasadena..." Hank says. I marvel at his temperament and his ability to interject humor in such a dire situation. Then he addresses our group, "Does anyone have a better idea than just rushing the airfield?"

One of the Marines steps forward. "Sir, I've been surveilling the airfield. May I suggest an alternate plan?"

"Absolutely," Hank responds.

"You have grenades," the Marine remarks. "One man, me for example, could probably creep undetected to where the planes are parked. Then create a diversion by tossing grenades under the planes and onto the tanker truck. While the gooks are running around trying to figure out what's going on, the rest of you could make it to the only functional plane left on the airfield and prepare for takeoff." After a pause, the Marine asks, "What do you think?"

Hank claps the Marine on the shoulder. "I like it…except for you offering to go. You and the rest are too weak from being in captivity. I'll be the one who creates the diversion."

"Oh, no you don't," I protest. "I should be the one to go. After all, Hank, you came on this safari because of me."

"Uh, not entirely." Hank looks at the other prisoners. "We made quite a catch! By the way, who's going to fly the plane if something happens to you?"

Dammit! Hadn't thought of that. Hank makes a good point, and I don't have a valid response.

"We don't have time to argue. Besides, *I'm* the self-appointed leader and I'm the one who calls the shots," Hank says with authority. "Now listen up! As soon as the first grenade explodes, follow Steve, and run like hell to the jet. I'll be right behind you tossing grenades like chickenfeed in my wake taking out the rest of their fleet. The unexpected attack and confusion should give us enough time to get airborne."

I look at Hank with deep concern. I'm not so sure he'll have enough time to clear the area. He must've noticed my expression.

"Hey, lighten up!" Hank says in a stern voice. "I'll make it to the plane. I can run like a cheetah with his tail on fire. You just take care of yourself and your cargo," Hank gives me an affectionate punch on the shoulder and slips off into the darkness.

A few minutes later, we see and hear an explosion. One of the planes lifts a few feet off the ground and we watch it disintegrate, spewing burning fragments everywhere. Moments later another plane joins the first. The Viet Cong race in all directions attempting to locate the source of the mayhem while at the same time trying to find a safe haven.

"Let's get moving!" I shout. The captives

don't need much coaxing. We race toward the jet. Every few seconds another plane blows up and it feels like the whole world is exploding behind us. The earth shakes when the tanker explodes and erupts into flames. As we race across the tarmac, I'm concerned about Hank and keep looking back hoping to spot him.

We make it to the jet without any injuries. As we're boarding, I direct everyone to store the weapons they confiscated when we left the temple in the rear of the aircraft. I tell them to leave the stairway down and the hatch open until Hank arrives.

I then make my way to the cockpit and prepare to start the engines. However, the instruments are all labeled in Vietnamese. *Damn the luck anyway!* I rush back to the cabin and signal for Cheyn, the Vietnamese interpreter, to come to the cockpit. When I explain the problem, he looks at the control panel and shakes his head.

"I don't read Vietnamese," he says. "I only speak it."

"Oh, great," I say and can't keep the exacerbation out of my voice. "Now what do we do?"

"I think Hai, the Vietnamese prisoner you released, can read Vietnamese," Cheyn says. "I'll get him."

Before Cheyn returns, I look out the side window and see Hank sprinting toward the plane. I also see two Marines at the bottom of the stairs covering Hank's escape with a couple of the weapons that were brought aboard. *Thank God!* I continue to watch, and as soon as Hank boards, the Marines follow and pull up the stairs, closing the hatch behind them.

Cheyn enters the cockpit with Hai in tow and between them they help me decipher the instrument panel. Before long, I'm confident I can fly this bird.

I request that the two of them remain in the front seats close to the cockpit where I have immediate access to them—at least for the time being. Both comply.

I engage the engines and begin to taxi toward the runway. In the meantime, a troop of enemy soldiers armed with automatic weapons have lined up across the tarmac attempting to block our path. *Fat chance! If they think a human blockade is going to stop a jet, they're sadly mistaken.* As I push the throttle forward and accelerate, they spray the plane with bullets. Their weapons are no match for the C-12, and apparently seeing they're failing in their quest, they jump to their feet and begin to scatter.

I'm a firm believer in payback, and sometimes I just can't help myself. This is one of those times.

Deliberately staying low, I buzz the runway just above their heads. Terrorized, they hit the tarmac face down, and plug their ears with their fingers. "This one's for the good ole U.S.A." I mutter. I resist the urge to turn and buzz them again—just for good measure.

Once we're airborne, apparently realizing we're finally safe, the freed prisoners begin to cheer. And who can blame them after spending weeks or months in a hellhole of a prison. I look out of the side window as we continue to climb and can see the entire airfield we just left. It's a blazing inferno and the petro escaping from the damaged planes gives the appearance of rivers of fire. From this altitude the men on the ground look like a swarm of confused ants running helter-skelter.

I swipe at the sweat dripping in my eyes. We escaped without a second to spare.

Su Lin?

• • •

I'm feeling more relaxed when I realize the C-12 handles a lot like Webb's Cessna which I had the privilege of flying on several occasions. And even though I'm unable to read the instrument panel, I have no trouble maneuvering the plane into the wild blue yonder as we head for more friendly skies.

Chapter Eleven

Harbor Lights

I can hardly believe we made it this far without so much as a broken fingernail. When I feel we're at a safe distance from Hanoi, I take time to study the maps which are stored in the side pocket of the pilot's seat. Even though they're printed in Vietnamese, the names of countries and cities on maps are universal. I'm also able to calculate distances with Hai's help. Thailand is only eight hundred miles from Hanoi.

From my military service, I know that Thailand is the nearest Asian country that is U.S. friendly and that there are American air and naval bases situated there. The Cho Phraya River is clearly defined on the map and flows from Hanoi past Thailand's capital, Bangkok. Cheyn informs me that, although Thai is the official language spoken in Thailand, many of the Thais speak English.

I set my heading and begin the search for the Cho Phraya River. Luckily, light from the full moon shimmers on the river and I follow its path toward Bangkok without having to use the instruments. Parker moves up the aisle and takes the copilot seat. Keeping my attention on the terrain, I say, "Welcome home, son."

Parker grasps my right forearm and blurts, "Thank you for being my dad and for saving all of us. I love you!" I don't want to lose him now that I've found him—for the second time—and I want to hold him and never let him go! However, I don't have that right nor do I want to interfere in his life or the lives of his adopted parents.

I'm moved to tears by his expression of love, but I'm too emotional and focused on the operation of the plane to immediately respond. When I finally have a moment, I glance at Parker. He's sound asleep. Yet, just having him beside me means the world to me. I'm eager to get to Bangkok so I can contact Niàn and Chi and put their minds at ease. I can only imagine what they're going through not knowing what's taking place a world away. However, I'm confident that Su Lin knows our son is now safe! Afterall, she helped pull the strings.

Parker stirs and returns to the cabin where there's more leg room for him to stretch out. The cabin becomes quiet, and I suspect the prisoners have succumbed to the peaceful slumber that has eluded them for much too long.

I jump when Hank sticks his head into the cockpit, "Nice work getting this show on the road!"

he shouts over the whir of the jets.

"You know I couldn't have done it without you!" I shout.

"Hell, man! That was my kind of rodeo. I had the time of my life back there. This experience will be the highlight of my memoirs," Hank retorts.

"Let's just hope nothing happens to eclipse this highlight. We're not out of the woods yet."

"Bring it on, pilgrim!" Hank snorts. "I think we could even give John Wayne a run for his money."

I just shake my head. When I glance back, Hank has already turned and headed back to the cabin area. I suspect he's going to join the others and catch some much-needed shuteye of his own.

• • •

I pray we're safe from enemy air attack. If what we just left was the only airfield in the vicinity, all the planes within striking distance were destroyed or severely damaged because of the havoc wrought by Hank's generous use of hand grenades. So, an air attack, doesn't appear imminent.

I don't need to read the instruments to navigate, and with Hai's help, I check the fuel gauge. It registers full. I reason that if Webb's Cessna can fly at this altitude and speed for about six hours so can the C-12. That's more than enough time to get us to Bangkok.

Having overcome all the obstacles thrown at us, I'm feeling confident of being able to land safely in Bangkok—especially if Su Lin continues to be our guiding light.

• • •

My complacency is soon shattered when I hear angry voices coming from the cabin. Before I can determine what's causing the ruckus, Hai bullies his way to the cockpit pushing Hank in front of him. He has Hank in a stranglehold and is threatening him with Hank's bayonet.

"You, pilot," Hai hisses, "do as I say or this one dies."

Stunned at the sudden turn of events, all I can manage is a weak, "Okay."

Hai shoves Hank down in the copilot seat and takes a position behind us, still wielding the bayonet. I reason the other passengers don't fire the weapons stored in the rear of the plane for fear of punching a hole in the cabin causing decompression of the aircraft. Also in such tight quarters, they could hit me or Hank.

"What is it you want?" I ask.

"Never mind! You just do as I say," Hai sneers.

Hai leans forward, and with the hilt of the knife, he shatters every display on the instrument panel. With a joker grin, he smirks, "What I want is for this plane to crash and all of you Americans die in retaliation for my countrymen you killed back there."

That's when it dawns on to me that Hai was probably a Cong plant used to spy on the American prisoners. Being segregated from the rest, he had special treatment and the guards had the opportunity to debrief him without the others knowing. *We didn't come this far to rescue the interpreters just to have them die at the hands of a traitor.* Just as I tense ready to take on Hai, Hank intervenes.

"Not on my watch!" Hank snarls and gives Hai a smart elbow to the ribs. Hai screams and doubles up falling to the floor. Hank is instantly on him, and they scuffle for a few moments in the close quarters of the passageway.

Hai is no match for Hank and never had a chance. In seconds, Hank has him in a hammer lock and jerks him to his feet. Hank's bayonet is lying a few feet from the scrimmage. Hank retrieves it and cuts the sleeves from Hai's shirt and tears them into strips. Using the strips, he binds Hai's hands and feet. Then with the help of other passengers, they shove Hai into the first passenger seat, tie him down, and gag him.

I've got my hands full flying the plane. However,

losing Hai as an interpreter doesn't bother me. I can fly without instruments and having the river as a guide and being close to our destination, we really don't need him or the instruments.

From previously studying the maps, I found that the Cho Phraya River intersects the Gulf of Thailand in the South China Sea. An hour or so after the encounter with Hai, and averting disaster, I see what appears to be the lights of a harbor in the distance. I summon Parker and ask him to return to the flightdeck.

"Where are we?" he asks as he gazes out of the plane.

"We're approaching Thailand, and I need your help to contact the tower in Bangkok."

In the past, I've taken Parker up in Webb's Cessna a few times so he's familiar with a cockpit and pilot lingo. My attention is focused on the terrain, and with the widespread presence of U.S. military bases, I assume there are English-speaking air controllers at the airport.

"Can you figure out how to use the headset to contact the airfield?" I ask Parker.

Parker eyes the destroyed instrument panel for a few moments and then unhooks one of the headsets and puts it on. He twists a few knobs that are still intact, and Thai chatter comes from his headset. Parker communicates in English and requests an English-speaking person to direct our landing. Almost instantly the conversation reverts to English.

"American C-12, this is the control tower at Bangkok. We have you on our radar and you are cleared to land."

Heart-stopping moments pass before I see in the distance the lights of a runway.

"Parker, you did it!" I shout.

"No, Dad. You and Hank did it. The rest of us are just along for the ride."

"Don't sell yourself short, we couldn't have done it without you and the others."

"And if it weren't for me and the others, you wouldn't have had to have become involved in the first place," Parker shoots back. "I got you into it, and the least I can do, is help find a way out!"

I nod and let it go.

Although I'm skilled enough to fly by the seat of my pants, I need to know wind direction, airspeed, and how to lower the landing gear. I ask Parker to request someone in the tower who can take us through the landing sequence step by step as we approach.

We wait a few minutes until finally someone from the tower says, "I'm familiar with the C-12.

I can talk you through the landing." With his help, the landing goes smoothly. When at last the wheels touch down and we taxi to the terminal, I sink back into the pilot's seat and breathe a sigh of relief. It's hard to believe we're finally safe. I announce to the passengers that we've landed on friendly soil, and once again the cabin is filled with cheering.

• • •

The controller at the Bangkok terminal must have alerted the American embassy of our incoming aircraft. An envoy from the American Embassy meets with us inside the terminal shortly after we deplane. The officer in charge identifies himself as United States Marine Sgt. Victor Courtney.

"Sirs," he begins, "welcome to Bangkok. I'm attached to the American Embassy guard detail and am here to escort you to the embassy. Ambassador Whitworth is awaiting your arrival."

Since Bangkok only became aware of our situation just before we landed, I'm stunned by the embassy's reception committee. "We just barely got here. How'd you know about us and our plight?" I ask.

"Sir, I'm not at liberty to reveal our source," Sgt. Courtney responds, "but our embassy was advised of the prison escape and the destruction of an airfield close to Hanoi almost as soon as the events took place. It was determined at a hastily called meeting with the local officials that, because of the proximity of the two incidents, they must be connected.

"Armed with that information, our ambassador concluded that the Americans being held prisoner by the Viet Cong in Hanoi had escaped. He also concluded the escapees must've highjacked a plane from the airfield and were headed for the nearest friendly country— Thailand. Ambassador Whitworth immediately dispatched an envoy from our embassy to meet you here, if indeed Bangkok was your destination." Sgt. Courtney pauses momentarily, snaps to attention, and renders a smart salute. "You're the epitome of patriotism and bravery. And let me be the first to salute you, sirs! I'm honored to be your escort."

I look at Hank, and in unison wc snap to attention and return Sgt. Courtney's salute.

• • •

When we exit the terminal, a bus is waiting to transport us to the American Embassy in Bangkok. When we arrive, Hank and I are ushered into an elaborate study to meet with the ambassador. The other Americans are escorted into a dining room at the embassy and served dinner. Hai is taken into custody.

During our meeting with the ambassador, Hank and I explain as best we can the circumstances surrounding our presence in a foreign, hostile country with which we are at war. Although the ambassador couldn't say so in words, it was evident he approved of our actions. We found out later that he requested no disciplinary action be taken against Hank or me regarding the Hanoi Hullabaloo—the name the Marines ultimately labeled the escape.

The interpreters and Marines, after they dined, were transported to an American barracks where they spent two days recuperating and being debriefed. They were given haircuts, provided with shaving equipment, and new uniforms before being flown to the United States.

The embassy also contacted the escapees' loved ones to ensure them that all were safe and would soon be back in the States. Since Parker and the other interpreters are government employees, they're kept with the group. And I don't mind being separated from him, knowing he's in safe hands.

Hai was transported to the States where he's awaiting trial for a myriad of war crimes all carrying prison sentences.

• • •

The ambassador provides Hank and me rooms in the American Embassy in Bangkok. We spend the next day catching up on sleep and recuperating. The afternoon of the second day, as we're strolling through the peaceful embassy garden, Hank stops me. "What's up, partner? You're acting pretty solemn considering the success of our mission."

I pull a leaf from a nearby rose bush and pretend to examine it to avoid Hank's gaze. Knowing Hank, he's not going to let the matter drop.

"Well?" he persists.

"Just thinking about Su Lin," I finally confess.

"I thought so," says Hank. "And in case you didn't realize it, we're only five hours, as the crow flies, from Shanghai."

Still studying the leaf, I ask, "What's your point?"

"Well, you need closure. Perhaps a trip to Wai Sang will provide the answers you're seeking."

"I'm not sure— ,"

"I am!" Hank interrupts. "We got to Shanghai once by pretending to be Chinese nationals returning to our homeland." He then asks, "You up to giving it another try?"

I toss the leaf into the air, "Hell yes, man!" I shout. "You'd take that risk again just for me?" I ask.

"Hell yes, man!" Hank replies mimicking my expression. "And besides, outwitting the opposition is invigorating. I welcome the challenge!"

I squint at him. "Looking for another chapter for your memoirs?"

The grin on his face stretches from ear to ear.

Resuming our walk, we head back toward the embassy, "You're good at reading my mind," I say, "How'd you know that I promised myself that if I survived the rescue, I'd revisit the hospital at Wai Sang?"

"I'm clairvoyant. And besides you're an open book when it comes to Su Lin. It's now or never," Hank says. "We damn sure ain't comin' back here in this lifetime." Then after a pause, Hank snorts, "C'mon, let's light this candle. I'm itchin' for some action before I get too old."

"You friggin' kiddin' me! At this rate, you won't live long enough to get old, much less *too* old."

• • •

The flight from Bangkok to Shanghai proceeds without a glitch. *We must be livin' right*, I think as we clear the terminal in Shanghai and hail a taxi. During the ride to Wai Sang, my brain is saturated with memories of the time I spent here over twenty years ago.

When the cab pulls up in front of the hospital, I'm suddenly overcome with sentimentality. Hank and I exit the cab and stand on the front walkway. Time has taken its toll, and nothing looks the same.

In fact, it appears the facility is abandoned and in the process of being demolished.

I look back and notice the cab is still at the curb. "Come on, Hank, let's go," I plead. "This wasn't such a good idea after all."

"We've come this far…" Hank starts to protest but I insist we leave. Before we can turn back, the taxi pulls away.

"Ni hao," says an elderly Chinese man as he approaches us from the back of the hospital. He looks vaguely familiar, and I recognize his voice. It's Hóng, the orderly who assisted me when I was a patient here all those years ago.

"Hóng?" I ask.

"Yes, it me," he replies and bows. "I know you. Captain Parker, yes?"

"It is me, and I assume you remember Hank?" I ask, and gesture toward Hank.

"I do," Hóng says and bows to Hank.

Hank returns the gesture. "What's going on here?" Hank asks looking around at the diminished condition of the hospital.

"Village of Wai Sang not spared from bombs. Some hit hospital," Hóng remarks. "No longer safe so take down."

"I see," I reply. "And Dr. Ming?"

"He go to big hospital in Shanghai. No one left

here," Hóng says and the sadness in his voice is unmistakable.

Standing here amid all the memories, I begin having flashbacks and am eager to distance myself from the past. "Thank you, Hóng," I say and turn toward the street in hopes of hailing another taxi or at least a rickshaw.

"No! You no go, you come with Hóng," Hóng insists.

I'm surprised at his insistence, which is much out of character. His impatience is evident, and not waiting for an answer, Hóng turns and starts toward the rear of the hospital.

"Don't think—" I start to protest. Hóng cuts me off.

"So sorry, Captain, you *must* come!" he says emphatically.

Hank already has me in tow, so I grudgingly trudge around to the back of the building.

"Okay, now what?" I grumble when we're in the garden.

"Me not *chi-sin*," Hóng remarks. "But must do what I promise."

Chi-sin is the Chinese word for crazy, and I'm perplexed at Hóng's actions. I fold my arms across my chest and wait.

"You come," Hóng insists and starts toward the

rear of the garden.

"Hóng, I'm not going one step further until you tell me what this is about," I demand.

Hóng turns back to me and blurts, "Su Lin come in my sleep. She know you come here. She say give you special bonsai."

I'm speechless. *Su Lin?* When I don't move, Hóng throws his hands up in apparent disgust and hurries to the bonsai portion of the garden. I'm stunned to learn that Hóng also has had visits from Su Lin.

A few minutes later, Hóng returns carrying one of the bonsai, Su Lin's favorite. When Hóng approaches and hands me the tree, I notice the trunk is a bit more gnarled with age, but overall, its shape hasn't changed much. My hands shake as I hold the tree and reverently gaze at it. *Some of Su Lin's ashes are in this container.*

"Now Su Lin no longer come. I live in peace," Hóng mumbles and rushes from the garden.

I'm astounded at Hóng's revelation that Su Lin also visited him in *his* sleep. This knowledge reinforces my belief that my Su Lin visitations were real and not just imagined. Wanting more details about Hóng's Su Lin's appearances, I shout, "Wait!"

"I no wait, I go," Hóng shouts back and sprints around the corner of the building. It's apparent that after fulfilling his obligation to Su Lin he doesn't want to talk to us any longer.

I look at Hank. He shrugs. "Looks like you and Hóng have been eating the same psychedelic mushrooms."

• • •

Hank and I return to the airport in Shanghai and take the next plane back to Bangkok. When we arrive at the embassy, we're informed that the freed prisoners have already been transported to the United States on a military plane. Hank and I schedule a commercial flight for the next day.

Before leaving the embassy, I ask the chef for a small container to carry the bonsai. He provides me with cardboard box just the right size for the tree if I leave the top open.

• • •

Once we're on the plane, I obey the flight attendant's instructions and place the box containing the bonsai under the seat in front of me. It's positioned where I can keep an eye on it. I stare out of the window at the landscape as we taxi to the runway preparing for takeoff. The pagoda-type buildings we pass remind me of the afternoon so long ago when, during one of our walks, I pointed to the sky and told Su Lin that someday I would take her up into the wild blue yonder. *Little did I suspect...*

Chapter Twelve

Imagination

When the interpreters arrive back in the United States, they're hospitalized for several days and given precautionary examinations. Being Parker's father, I'm privy to the nature of the exams. At the conclusion of a battery of tests, all three interpreters are released with a clean bill of health and resume their duties at the Pentagon.

Hank and I return to the airfield in Charleston where Webb welcomes us back with warm greetings. We spend our first afternoon catching up. Webb appears intrigued by the story of our journey, and Hank and I spend an hour or so taking turns filling him in on all the sordid details.

"Wish I could've been part of the action," Webb comments. "I miss it, but you two paint a pretty vivid picture." He then emits a hearty laugh and points the matchstick he'd been chewing on in my direction. "Wish I could've seen your face when the snake dropped on you!"

"The snake!" I shout. "We flew into a hostile country, forged our way through a booby-trapped, bug-infested jungle, stormed a temple, and fought off well-armed Cong guards. After rescuing ten Americans and one Vietnamese, who turned out to be a traitor, we hiked back through the jungle to an enemy airfield where we destroyed seven aircraft on the ground and hijacked a plane from under the noses of the enemy. Once we were airborne, we were accosted by the traitor, who tried to hijack our plane and cause it to crash…and you're intrigued by a snake?"

Hank rolls his eyes in mock disgust just as my phone rings.

"Hello," I answer.

"Steve," Niàn says and I instantly have a queasy feeling in the pit of my stomach.

"Everything all right?" I ask.

"Not sure," Niàn replies. "Parker called today. His voice sounded strained, so I asked him if he was all right. He said he's been having severe headaches, nightmares, and spells of amnesia."

A cold fear grips me as I remember having read that the Cong were into brainwashing using drugs and hypnosis. "Did he say what kind of nightmares?"

"Nothing specific. He sounded like he did as a child when he had bad dreams." Niàn pauses, "Steve, my gut tells me something is very wrong."

"I'm on my way." When I hang up, I explain

to Hank and Webb the circumstances. I feel guilty leaving them in the lurch, but my son comes first. I tell them so.

Webb doesn't miss a beat. "Hank," he says, "you go with Steve. I'm okay here since we have the two extra pilots."

Hank nods, "Great idea, Webb," he says and looks at me for affirmation.

At this point a myriad of emotions is driving the bus and all I can manage is a weak "Thanks."

Webb says, "It's an eight-hour drive from here to Herndon. Time may be of the essence so take the Cessna. Just had her inspected and refueled, so she's ready to go."

When I try to speak, I choke up. Webb waves us on as he says, "Go on, get outta here!"

• • •

We rent a car at the airport when we land at Dulles, and Hank and I drive to the Zhēn residence. Both Niàn and Chi meet us at the door. It's obvious Chi has been crying and worry lines crease Niàn's brow.

"Come in," Niàn says as he swings the door open wide. Chi has a carafe of coffee and a tray of cookies laid out, and the four of us take seats around the table.

As Chi busies herself pouring coffee, I look at

Niàn and say, "Tell us what's been going on."

Niàn stirs the coffee around in his cup taking a moment before answering. "It started almost as soon—"

"Wait!" I interrupt. "What started?"

"Oh, sorry, Niàn remarks. "I'm getting the carriage before the horse, as you Americans say. Parker spent a couple of nights here in his old bedroom before returning to his duties at the Pentagon. During his stay, he kept complaining about headaches. We attributed them to his being stressed and having been held captive in a foreign country. We almost dismissed that theory when his screams woke us in the middle of the night."

"What frightened him?" Hank asks, and the concern in his voice is evident.

"When we asked him, he couldn't remember the dream, only that it was terrible," Chi interjects with a forlorn look in her eyes. "I held him in my arms to comfort him and he clung to me just like he did when he had bad dreams as a child."

Eager to get answers, I ask, "Any idea what could've caused his distress?"

"None!" Niàn says fielding the question. "He spent almost every other weekend here at home and appeared to be normal. That was before he was dispatched to Vietnam." After a pause, he says in a hushed tone, "Steve, something terrible happened to him in Vietnam. We don't have a clue, and Chi and I are devastated. Think you can you help us?"

"If I have to move heaven and earth!"

"Make that if we have to move heaven and earth," Hank exclaims.

Relieved to have Hank onboard, I then ask, "Where's Parker?"

"He's coming back here tomorrow morning to spend the weekend and should be here by lunch time. When he heard you and Hank were coming, he seemed to cheer up. It's only a thirty-minute drive, but with the weekend traffic, it'll take longer." Niàn looks at Chi before continuing. "We thought it best not to let him know we were going to tell you about his...his condition. We figured he might be more guarded if he knew that you knew he was having problems."

"I agree," I say, and looking at Hank, add, "We'll act like this is just a casual visit." Hank nods.

"I've prepared the guest room for you," Chi says. "So sorry, we only have one but it has twin beds so you should be comfortable enough."

"Uh, I don't want to impose so I'll—" Hank starts to say but I cut him off midsentence.

"Look, partner, you're not imposing! I just recently spent a hellacious couple of days and nights in the jungle with you, so I think you can spend a couple of nights in the guest room with me." Hank looks sheepish, "You're as much a family member as I am so get over it, already!"

I'm embarrassed when I notice the startled expression on Chi and Niàn's faces and regret my outburst. "Sorry, buddy," I say to Hank. "I don't think you realize how much you're appreciated. You, and you alone, got me through the rescue operation and I owe you a great deal…a debt I can never repay. Don't ever undersell yourself. Having you at my side with your experience and expertise in making critical decisions has been a blessing. We need you now more than ever." I pause before adding, "Will you forgive me?"

"Nothing to forgive," Hank says. Then clearing his throat, he adds, "I didn't have much of a family-life and I'm pretty clumsy around people and feel like I'm always in the way—"

Niàn takes the reins. "Chi and I being foreigners can sympathize with your feelings. We've been there," he says and nods toward Chi. "However, let me assure you you're just as much a part of Parker's family as we are. Parker has been blest with not only another father but an uncle, whom he adores, as well. So as Steve so aptly puts it, get over it, already!"

Chi delivers the parting shot. "Anyone want

more coffee?" she asks as she holds up the carafe. "This will either help settle the nerves or aggravate them!"

We all smile. *Clearly, we're all in this together!*

• • •

After dinner when we're alone in our room, Hank says, "You sure know how to hurt a guy."

"Yep, and if you try to weasel out on me again, you'll feel real pain! I learned a few tricks in Vietnam, so don't tempt me," I whip into a karate stance.

"Wow! You're real scary. No wonder that snake jumped over the side of the boat when it saw you," Hank retorts. "Facing you was a fate worse than death!"

"Kidding aside, Hank, you've been my rudder as well as my stabilizer. And I meant it when I said I couldn't have come this far without you, so resign yourself, you're in for the long haul."

I thought I detected tears in Hank's eyes when he gave me a salute before turning over in his bed. I know I'm a basket case when it comes to Parker. But didn't know Hank felt the same way. *Good old Hank!*

"Aren't you going to kill the lights?" Hank asks.

"Afraid of the dark!" I respond. "I'll turn them down, but not out!"

●●●

The next afternoon when Parker arrives, I'm stunned by his appearance. He's lost weight. He's haggard and his hair and clothing are disheveled. Dark circles underscore his bloodshot eyes and his lips have what appears to be an involuntary quiver. He isn't the same Parker we rescued only a couple of short weeks ago.

When we embrace, he seems tense. "Parker! How've you been?" I ask, hoping he'll open up.

He pushes me aside and looks away. "I'm okay!" He then asks Chi, "What's for lunch, Mom?" and heads toward the kitchen.

I look at Hank. Parker completely ignores Hank, which is out of character. Hank follows him into the kitchen.

"Hey, buddy," Hank says. "Don't I get a hug?"

Parker turns. "Oh, yeah. Good to see you again." He makes no move to hug Hank. Instead, he eyes the spread on the table.

Lunch is strained and Niàn, Chi, Hank, and I engage in light chit-chat. Parker keeps his focus on the food and sidesteps answering any questions or taking part in the conversation.

After lunch, Niàn pats his breast pocket where he keeps his cigarettes and suggests we go out to the patio for in some fresh air and sunshine. Chi is already clearing the dishes and Hank is helping, so Niàn, Parker, and I go outside. It's a perfect autumn day and we sit around a glass top table in the shade. Niàn lights a cigarette and rears back in his chair. He looks relaxed, although I know he's wrestling with a jumble of emotions, as am I.

I notice movement in the sky and when I look up, I see hundreds of starlings coming together in the cloudless sky. I've watched the birds on numerous occasions and each time I do, I'm captivated by the way they seem to synchronize their movements. They whirl in unison creating swirling patterns, and then as if on cue, they twist and turn as they swoop and soar overhead. Watching them is fascinating.

I point to the airshow and remark, "The way the birds move through the air reminds me, although not in color, of a kaleidoscope I had as a kid…"

Parker becomes rigid, and I notice he has a glazed look in his eyes. After a moment, he starts to speak in Chinese. Niàn is on his feet rushing around the table. He kneels beside Parker, who appears to be in a trance of some kind. *Hypnosis?* I don't interfere not wanting to interrupt the scene unfolding before me. *This may be a clue to unlock the mystery of Parker's strange behavior.* After several minutes of nonstop rhetoric, Parker abruptly stops speaking and slumps back into his chair.

Looking at me, Niàn asks, "What happened?" as he tries to rouse Parker.

I reach over and take Parker's wrist. His breathing and pulse both seem normal.

"I'm not sure but from what I observed, Parker appeared to be in a hypnotic state when he spoke," I respond. "I don't want to alarm you but before going to Vietnam I read some articles that implied the Cong were using drugs and hypnosis on prisoners. The theory was that the captives, upon release, would be implanted in strategic government facilities to be used as Trojan Horses." I pause long enough for my statement to sink in and then ask Niàn to explain to me what Parker was saying.

Niàn slowly goes back to his chair and fumbles in his pocket for a cigarette. His hands shake as he lights it. "He seemed to be relating a conversation between the Chinese ambassador and the U.S. Secretary of War," Niàn says. "I recognized who they were when Parker spoke their names."

I think about it for a moment. "That would certainly square with the Trojan Horse theory. Niàn, I think the boys were kidnapped in Vietnam to be used in an experiment. They were chosen because of their government positions and access to private meetings within the War Department.

"I've read some articles on the use of hypnosis

and drugs. My theory is that the interpreters were hypnotized by their captors to react to a buzzword. When the word is spoken, the interpreters go into a trance and relay the conversations of the meetings between the U.S. War Department, and the Chinese, Russian, and Vietnamese representatives to an enemy plant. Then, to receive the information from the interpreters, all the enemy plants need to do is say the magic word and it's as though they were present in person at the meetings. The plants can activate the communication over the phone or by meeting the interpreters somewhere in person. You know the old saying, 'forewarned is forearmed.' We just accidently stumbled on the buzzword and Parker responded."

"This is all so confusing…what is a buzzword?" Niàn asks and frowns.

"It's American slang for a trigger, so to speak. When the unsuspecting person hears the word, he responds in the same manner as Parker just did. Now we must figure out what the word is to get him deprogrammed. Do you remember what we were talking about immediately before Parker went into a trance?"

Niàn furrows his brow. "I believe you were talking about the birds," he remarks and looks skyward.

I follow his gaze, "Okay, do you recall what I said?" "Yes, because you used a word I didn't recognize and wanted to ask you about later. It sounded like kideskop or something like that," Niàn answers.

Kaleidoscope! "Now I remember!" I blurt. "I think I know the word. However, I don't want to say it out loud for fear of what it might do to Parker if it is the buzzword. He seems to be coming out of the trance."

Parker blinks several times, opens his eyes and looks around, "Man, I must've fallen asleep. Didn't know I was so tired."

I'm relieved that Parker has returned to a semblance of normal. "Having been held prisoner, you've been through a lot," I say, "and your body and mind need time to recoup."

Niàn nods. Just then, the sliding glass door between the kitchen and patio slides open. We look up and see Chi and Hank coming out to join us.

Rubbing his eyes, Parker stands and remarks, "Think I'll go lie down for a while. I feel safe and comfortable here at home." We all watch him retreat into the house. Hank and Chi both look at us with questioning eyes.

A few moments after Parker leaves, Niàn says, "Let's go to the gazebo. The bonsai should be watered, and we can discuss the dilemma we face when Parker is unable to hear us."

The moment we enter the gazebo, Chi can wait no longer. "What dilemma!" she demands.

Niàn looks at me and nods, a signal for me to explain the situation. Chi must've also noticed the interaction. She grabs my hand and pleads, "What's wrong with Parker?"

Hank motions for Chi to take a seat on the swing. He chooses a side chair. They both look at me with expectation in their eyes.

I begin, "Almost as soon as we were seated on the patio, I looked up and spotted a flock of starlings soaring overhead. I commented that the way they swirled in synchronized patterns reminded me of a *kaleidoscope* I had as a kid."

Niàn approaches carrying a watering can and methodically begins to sprinkle each bonsai. I pause and watch him for a few moments.

"What's that got to do with Parker?" Chi demands and starts to rise. I detect the impatience in her voice and Hank puts his hand on her arm to calm her.

"I'm sorry, Chi, to take so long but everything happened so fast, I'm trying to put the events in sequence to give you a comprehensive picture." I continue, "As soon as I finished my statement regarding the birds, Parker became rigid and his eyes glaze. He then began reciting what Niàn recognized as a possible conversation between a Chinese representative and a representative from our War Department."

"What!" Chi exclaims. Standing, she starts to pace around the gazebo wringing her hands.

"Hold on! Let me explain my theory," I say. "Knowing what I know about the Cong using drugs and hypnosis on their prisoners, I think Parker and the other two interpreters were hypnotized and programmed to be spies after they were kidnapped. And if you think about it, it only makes sense that they were probably targeted from the time they were transported to Vietnam to translate at the summit. Programming three American citizens, who just happen to be government employees, to send back to the U.S. to use as spies and report on conversations between foreign representatives and the War Department was nothing short of genius. And the implementation was so skillful, it was just pure luck we were able to figure it out." I pause and shake my head, trying to formulate my theory so Chi will understand it.

"I suspect that during the hypnosis while in captivity, the interpreters were indoctrinated with a buzzword and conditioned to respond to that buzzword by reciting minutes to their handlers of the private meetings. Having spies in the Pentagon to report on upcoming war strategy would give the Cong a definite advantage. The exchanges between the interpreters and their handlers could be done over the phone or by meeting somewhere in person."

Then I explain, "In order to accomplish their mission, the Cong would have to pick an English word that all three would understand and one that wasn't used often, if at all in this day and age, so as not to trigger the hypnotic state accidentally during casual conversation. I believe the word *kaleidoscope* is the trigger—for Parker anyway."

I stop long enough to give Hank and Chi time to assimilate the information.

"Well, I'll be damned," Hank finally mummers.

Chi has stopped pacing. "Now that we know what the problem is, how do we fix Parker?" she asks.

"I've been thinking about that," I respond. "For now, we do nothing, and for heaven's sake, do not use the word *kaleidoscope* in Parker's presence." I look at Hank, "Since Herndon is so close to the Pentagon, I suggest we call first thing Monday and set up an appointment with an official in the War Department. I think that may be the best place to start. With all the modern advances in medicine and technology, the government may already have a system in place to address these situations."

"That will take time! What about Parker in the here and now?" Chi exclaims.

"In order to help Parker, we must get an expert on board. We'll know more after meeting with the War Department on Monday. If we try anything on our own, we may do more harm than good. It's important that in the meantime, we pretend nothing is wrong."

During our entire conversation, Niàn has been quietly standing by and I'm surprised when he suddenly blurts, "I want to be in on that meeting at the Pentagon!"

"I think you being there is an excellent idea," I comment. "You have firsthand experience with Parker's nightmares, which will come in handy when we try to explain the situation to the brass."

"Plus being confronted by two concerned fathers may carry some weight as far as getting an interview with one of the higher-ups," Hank remarks.

"Throw in one concerned uncle, and I'd dare them to dismiss us without a hearing," I add. Hank smiles and gives me a thumbs-up.

• • •

Although Sunday is tense, Niàn and Chi play

their roles to perfection. If Parker notices anything different, he doesn't let on. It's close to 7:00 p.m. by the time we finish dinner. After we help clear the table, Parker says, "I feel rested after that long afternoon nap, so if it's okay with you, Mom, I think I'll head back to D.C. and avoid the Monday morning traffic."

Chi glances at Niàn and he nods. "Good idea," she says. "You're getting so thin, I baked some of your favorite cookies and fixed a some for you to take back." She hurries to the kitchen and returns with a plastic container.

"Thanks, Mom," Parker says. He leans down and gives Chi a kiss on the forehead.

We walk Parker to his vehicle, and I notice Chi's farewell embrace is more intense than normal. I catch her eye and shake my head, hoping she'll get my message and not appear overly concerned. She responds with a slight smile.

Standing in the driveway, we watch Parker back out into the street and speed away giving us a vague wave. When we return to the house, Niàn remarks, "Since it's Sunday, we can't contact the Pentagon until tomorrow morning to schedule an appointment, and then who knows how long we'll have to wait. D.C. is only a thirty-minute drive from here and I've been thinking that if we show up early tomorrow morning, even without an appointment, we'll have a better chance of being heard sooner than later."

"You make a good point," I respond. "And if we fail and must wait to see someone, so be it! I can outwait the best of 'em," I say and look at my watch. It's 7:45. "Don't know about the rest of you, but I'm beat. I suggest we get some sleep if we're going to hit it early tomorrow morning. We certainly want to bring our A-game to this meeting."

• • •

We're awakened by a rainstorm early Monday morning. I look at my watch, it's almost 5:00. Hank and I quickly dress and join Niàn and Chi in the kitchen. The aroma of bacon frying makes my mouth water.

"Good morning," Niàn says and sets the newspaper aside.

Chi wipes her hands on her apron and takes two mugs from an overhead cabinet. Hank steps up, "Let me do that," he says and gently takes the mugs from her. She smiles and nods. Bringing the mugs to the table, Hank pours coffee for the two of us. He then holds up the pot offering to refill Niàn's cup. Niàn shakes his head. "If I drink too much, I have to make too many pit stops."

Chi joins us, carrying plates of bacon and eggs

with sides of buttered toast. As we eat breakfast, Niàn says, "We're starting early enough to beat most of the Monday morning traffic." Emptying his juice glass, he places his napkin on the table. "I'm ready anytime you are."

Cramming the last bite of bacon into his mouth, Hank remarks, "I'm ready."

"Let's go!" I say and we all head for the door.

Chi walks with us and the forlorn expression in her eyes saddens me. I take her hands in mine, "We'll get it figured out, Chi. Never doubt that!"

• • •

Upon arriving at the Pentagon, we soon find that gaining an audience with an official is not a simple matter. A friendly receptionist greets us in the front lobby. The name plate displayed on a half-circle counter-type desk identifies her as Michelle. However, when we ask to see someone in charge, she hesitates. It appears she has a script to address visitors who just walk in unannounced. She explains we must first have an appointment and that tours must be scheduled fourteen days in advance.

Since I'm the biological father, I take the lead. "I appreciate your position," I say in an authoritative manner. "However, this isn't about a tour or a casual visit, it's a matter of national security." When she rolls her eyes, I become more aggressive. Gesturing to Hank and Niàn I remark, "Rest assured, we're not terrorists or kooks. I'm Captain Steven Parker, retired Navy pilot." I extract my wallet from my rear pants pocket and show her my driver's license which has a veteran's status symbol on it proving my military service. I then introduce Hank and he follows suit by showing Michelle his driver's license with the same veteran's military symbol. "We have a legitimate concern, and it could turn into an international crisis if not addressed immediately!"

The look on my face, the determination in my voice, our ex-military service status, or all the above must've made an impression on Michelle.

She points to chairs in the reception area. "Take a seat. I'll get someone to help you."

I take a seat where I can see Michelle. I'm not sure if it's a stall or not. I watch her make several calls apparently attempting to find someone to escort us into the facility. After a fifteen-minute wait, a distinguished-looking gentleman heads in our direction, flanked by two uniformed Marines with sidearms attached to their duty belts.

"Mr. Parker," he says as he approaches.

I stand. "That's me."

"I'm Randal Cassidy, secretary to General Thomas Warner. How may I assist you?"

I introduce Hank and Niàn and explain who they are in relation to the pending problem. "Our son, Parker Zhēn, is one of your interpreters."

"Yes, I know Parker. Now what's this all about?" Cassidy demands and the impatience in his voice is evident.

Cassidy's attitude rankles me, and my patience is now wearing thin. "Is there someplace more private where we can discuss this issue?" I ask.

Cassidy must have picked up on my mood and points to a small conference room adjacent to the reception area. When we enter, the two Marines remain outside standing guard at the door. "I'm a busy man so if you don't mind…" Cassidy begins as soon as we're seated around a small conference table.

Fed up with his attitude and the assertion of how important *he* is, I snarl, "Well, you're about to get a hell of a lot busier." Cassidy immediately puffs up, looking like he's ready to take me on, so I make the first move and lean across the table, getting in his face. As I do so, one of the guards, apparently watching through the glass office window, opens the door and steps in.

Cassidy holds up a restraining hand and the guard retreats. "I'm listening," Cassidy announces. Now that I have his attention, I say, "We have proof that our national security is being breached." I pause for a breath then continue, "And if you're not interested, I'm sure with our combined military service," I gesture to Hank and then back to me, "we can get an appointment with the guy in the White House."

Cassidy looks at the three of us with scorn in his eyes. "And just how is it you have proof of a breach?" he shoots back.

His holier-than-thou attitude changes as I relate the events that brought us here.

"Holy Mother of God," he mumbles when I finish my dissertation.

Apparently unable to wait any longer, Niàn jumps into the mix. It's obvious he's eager for a solution to Parker's problem. "Now, how can you help our son?" he demands.

Cassidy slumps back in his chair looking like a whipped pup. "Mr. Zhēn, I sympathize with you and wish there was an easy answer. What you've just told me is a concept we became aware of when it was used by North Korea during the Korean war. Our department keeps up with current infiltration practices and procedures as a matter of course. I'm not at liberty to discuss the countermeasures our country uses to protect its secrets. I can tell you that as part of my job I have been exposed to abuses by nonfriendly nations involving the use of hypnosis in obtaining classified or top-secret information. Nothing has recently surfaced to indicate the practice is currently being used by the Viet Cong. That's not to say that it isn't.

"In retrospect, I would assume that finding out we were sending American interpreters to the summit probably planted the idea when the Cong realized how they could easily resurrect the practice. I will make solving this a priority."

"And what do we do in the meantime?" Niàn asks.

"I'm sorry to say I don't have an answer to that either," Cassidy responds, and I notice his attitude has changed drastically. "How many people know about this?"

"As far as we know, only the three of us and Mrs. Zhēn," I reply. "We, of course, can't speak for the other two interpreters, Cheyn Hoser and Ivan Procoff."

"Of course. However, since Parker wasn't and isn't aware of his situation, it's likely the other two aren't either. Otherwise, they probably would have alerted us. This is a delicate matter and for the sake of the interpreters, I'm asking you keep this under wraps until we can come up with a solution." Rubbing the back of his neck, Cassidy adds, "I know that's asking a lot, but as you aptly pointed out, our country's security may be at risk."

"Even though I'm an immigrant, this is now my country," Niàn exclaims, "so yes, we will comply with your wishes."

Cassidy stands. "Gentlemen, thank you for coming forward." After an awkward moment, he continues, "It's not easy for me to take my pride in my hands, but I feel I owe all of you an apology. As you can imagine, we get many unsubstantiated claims and I spend a lot of time separating fact from fiction." Extending his hand to each of us, he says, "Please accept my apology."

We rise and take turns shaking his hand indicating no hard feelings. Cassidy walks us through the reception area to the exit, and after scribbling something on his business cards, he gives each of us one. "Until you hear otherwise, continue to treat Parker as if nothing is amiss. I promise you this will receive top priority. Please feel free to call me on my private line anytime." He points to the handwritten number on the back of the cards. "I will keep you informed of the progress as we move forward."

Chapter Thirteen

That Old Black Magic

On our return trip to Herndon, we engage in a lively discussion and decide Cassidy is what he purports to be and can be trusted. It's obvious, he has to be careful about what he can disclose and what he can't. We conclude that much of what he knows, is top secret and classified information.

"What do you think is going to happen?" Niàn asks as he exits onto the ramp leading to Virginia.

"Now that Cassidy has been made aware of the situation," Hank answers, "it's just a matter of wait and see. I remember Steve commenting earlier that he had read about the use of hypnosis and illegal drugs on war prisoners to obtain information. If Steve and the public are aware of the infiltration attempts, then our government would most certainly be aware. Cassidy may be sandbagging us to keep from compromising intelligence and counterintelligence. How does he know from our brief meeting if we are friend or foe? As enterprising as our country is, it most certainly has an antidote in place as part of its protocol."

"I agree," I say. "Our country is usually on the

cutting edge of technology in every field. After talking to Cassidy, I'm feeling better about Parker and the other two being in good hands. It's a cinch none of us knows where to begin."

When we return to Herndon, it's early enough in the afternoon for Hank and me to fly back to Charleston. We pick up our rental car at the Zhēns and head back to Dulles, leaving Niàn to explain to Chi what happened at the Pentagon.

"It's best I do it alone," Niàn says. "Chi gets embarrassed when she becomes emotional."

"Just let her know we've set the wheels in motion and judging from the way Cassidy reacted, I think we'll have a solution in the not too distant future," says Hank.

• • •

Three days after returning to Charleston, I'm in our office at the airport when I receive a call. The caller is Cassidy, I motion Hank to my side and hold the phone in a position where he can also hear the conversation.

"Captain Parker," Cassidy begins, "first, let me assure you I found out that we do have the ability to deprogram the interpreters. Our inhouse psychiatrist, Dr. Amos Tekoa, better known among his colleagues as Dr. TK, explained the process to me. In a nutshell, hypnosis regression is a technique that can reverse any previous suggestions given under hypnosis. Since we know the trigger word is *kaleidoscope*, which incidentally was determined to work on all three interpreters, Dr. TK said the process would be quick and easy. That being said," Cassidy continues, "I've been asked to run something past you and all the other parents."

"Okay." I shrug as I look at Hank.

"After explaining the circumstances of the kidnapping and the hypnosis process to the director," Cassidy says, "the director was astonished that he wasn't aware of the process. He immediately arranged a meeting with the Secretary of Defense, who also wasn't aware that hypnosis was being used on prisoners. If you hadn't accidentally stumbled on it, no telling how many other POWs would have been programmed and integrated as unwitting spies. Your quick response may have saved many lives. Thank you again for your persistence."

Before I can respond, Cassidy rushes on. "The long and short of it is, the War Department would like to take advantage of the Cong kidnapping, hypnotizing, and using our citizens against their own country to advance the Cong's agenda. Since we're now informed and in control, the consensus is to take advantage of the situation. The plan we're proposing is to turn the Cong's weapon back on them by arranging fake meetings wherein we would give the interpreters faulty information to forward to the enemy. Our hope is that the false information would give the allies an advantage."

I glance at Hank. His expression is noncommittal. Needing time to think it through, I say, "I'm not so sure Niàn and Chi Zhēn would agree—"

Cassidy interrupts. "Tell the Zhēns the process would not be an experiment. The interpreters have already undergone the experimental phase foisted on them by the Cong. Our participation would be a onetime operation, not an experiment. Once it's used, of course, the opposition would be on the alert. Realizing we're on to their game, hopefully they would discontinue their use of drugs and hypnosis on other prisoners. We will, if you and the other parents agree to the deceit, proceed with the deprogramming immediately afterwards."

Damn good strategy if it works. However, I'm still leery of the concept, so I ask, "How would you proceed?"

"Quite obviously the interpreters are not aware they were hypnotized and will not be informed of the planned deceit. We will set up fake meetings between War Department personnel and plants posing as Chinese, Russian, and Vietnamese representatives. The meetings will proceed in the manner in which the interpreters are accustomed. However, the difference is we will use our people, posing as the foreign representatives. The plants will be given a prepared script—one we will design to confuse the opposition," Cassidy replies. "When our interpreters report the minutes of the meetings to their handlers, they will pass on the false information."

Clever idea! "I'll discuss it with the Zhēns," I say, "and let you know as soon as possible." Hank nods. He apparently thinks it's a good idea as well because he gives me a thumbs-up.

• • •

When I end the call with Cassidy, I call Niàn. After I explain the War Department's request, Niàn asks, "Why do they need *our* permission?"

"Since the boys are civilian employees and not even under contract, I don't think legally they do." I answer. "However, I feel, out of a sense of decency and respect for us, is the reason why they're asking. After all, we're the ones who brought the situation to their attention in the first place." After a pause, I ask, "What do you think?"

Long moments pass before Niàn replies, "Before coming to America, Chi and I lived under a dictatorship. We had no rights. Chinese lived and died at the whim of those in power. Life was and still is cheap.

"Living in America we've been exposed to a different way of life—one worth fighting for and dying for if it comes to that. Mr. Cassidy assured us Parker would be in good hands and I believe him. The interpreters' lives apparently would not be in danger and if the plan works and the allies gain even an inch of advantage, it would be worth the deceit. We, Chi and I, owe our adopted country our loyalty and now that we have an opportunity to repay even a small portion of what we received, we are more than willing to do so. I speak for both Chi and me when I say we agree."

Niàn has a way of putting things in perspective. "I'll let Cassidy know we are all in agreement," I say. "I'll keep you posted."

• • •

We don't expect to hear anything back right away, so we anxiously wait to see if the scheme worked. A week after his initial call, I receive a call from Cassidy. "Captain Parker, I have some good news for you and the Zhēns. The plan we devised worked flawlessly, and because they were unaware of the deceit, the Cong let their guard down and the allies were able to recapture a strategic base."

"That's wonderful. How about the interpreters?"

I ask.

"All three have been deprogrammed and were never informed they had been hypnotized or of the deceit. Dr. TK informed us it would be unwise to tell them because it might cause them unnecessary anxiety. As far as the interpreters know, the meetings were business as usual."

"I'll pass on the information to the Zhēns. Thank you," I respond and breathe a sigh of relief.

Chapter Fourteen

Till the End of Time

I stare at the ceiling in my hospital room. Having been diagnosed with terminal pancreatic cancer, and given less than a month to live, I mentally examine my life. I'm now sixty-three years old and conclude there's not much I would've done differently. I'm proud of my service to my country, I don't regret having loved Su Lin, and my son is a shining example of what America is all about.

Lost in my reverie, I'm suddenly jerked back to reality when someone raps on my open door. I look up and see Hank standing in the doorway.

"Hey, buddy. How goes the battle?" he asks as he approaches my bed.

"The good guys are winning," I reply.

"That's the spirit," he responds.

After an awkward silence, I say, "Hank, I know I can trust you. I have only one last request I'd like you to oversee."

"Whatever you want, just name it!" he replies.

"I hope you don't think I've gone over the edge when I ask you this. I assure you I'm as sane as you…oops, maybe that's not such a good comparison."

"Well, the fact that you can still insult me is a good sign," he says and chuckles. "What's this mysterious request?"

"Just hear me out before you try to reason with me, will you?" I ask.

"For you, the world."

"You should've told me that thirty some-odd years ago," I reply and manage a grin. "Now for my request. You know the story of Mǎ Lee, Su Lin's sister, putting ashes on the bonsai—"

"Indeed, I do! She thought since the tree could live a thousand years, by sprinkling some of Su Lin's ashes in the soil, Su Lin would also live a thousand years."

"You got it!" I reply. "In keeping with the Mǎ Lee tradition, I want to be cremated and have you put a tiny bit of my ashes on the same tree, the one I keep in my kitchen window. Don't think the procedure is a legitimate Chinese ritual. Mǎ Lee probably conceived of it on her own. However, I like the concept and the rite makes sense to me. I want to be with Su Lin, wherever she is."

"But—" Hank starts to say.

I interrupt. "You said you'd hear me out, remember? I'm not finished. After you comply with my request, see that Parker gets the tree. He knows how to care for bonsai. And when you tell him both his biological parents are a part of the tree, the Chinese in him will honor my request. Hopefully, he'll pass the bonsai on to his children, and they'll pass it on to their children, and the tree will thrive for at least a thousand years."

"That's a lot to hope for," Hank says. "Sprinkling ashes is probably against the law, but I will because I meant it when I said *for you the world*. Hank pulls his chair close to my bedside before continuing. "Being raised Christian, you realize a thousand years is just a drop in the bucket. What about the rest of eternity?"

"You're so cynical," I say. "Referring to the *rest* of something that has no beginning or end is an oxymoron. Besides, I'll cross that bridge when I come to it."

"Be that as it may," Hank says, "I'm going to hedge your bets and see that a priest administers the last rites—just in case. That may make crossing that bridge when you come to it a lot easier."

I'm touched by Hank's concern for my immortal soul. "Thanks, buddy," was all I could manage without breaking down.

• • •

With the help of a twenty-dollar bill, Hank coerces the mortician into giving him a teaspoon-size amount of Steve's ashes before the urn is sealed. After the funeral, armed with a plastic sandwich bag containing the ashes, Hank retrieves the bonsai from Steve's kitchen window and gently carries it out to the patio. Eager to fulfill his morbid promise, he places the tree on the patio table and is in the process of sprinkling the ashes into the pot when a shadow passes over head.

Hank glances up just as a rose finch flutterers down and perches on the wrought iron railing surrounding the patio. Familiar with the rose finch from having lived in China for several years, and knowing the rose finch is not indigenous to North America, Hank is intrigued. And even more so as he watches another rose finch join the first. They linger for a moment cocking their heads as they watch Hank. They then fly away together.

Well, I'll be damned!

About The Authors

Judith Blevins' whole professional life has been centered in and around the courts and the criminal justice system. Her experience in having been a court clerk and having served under five consecutive district attorneys in Grand Junction, Colorado, has provided the fodder for her novels. She has had a daily dose of mystery, intrigue and courtroom drama over the years, and her novels share all with her readers. In addition to the ten novels in **The Childhood Legends Series**®, she has authored or co-authored twenty-five adult novels.

Carroll Multz, a trial lawyer for over forty years, a former two-term district attorney, assistant attorney general, and judge, has been involved in cases ranging from municipal courts to and including the United States Supreme Court. His high-profile cases have been reported in the **New York Times**, **Redbook Magazine** and various police magazines. He was one of the attorneys in the **Columbine Copycat Case** that occurred in Fort Collins, Colorado, in 2001 that was featured by Barbara Walters on **ABC's 20/20**. He recently retired as an Adjunct Professor at Colorado Mesa University in Grand Junction, Colorado, where he taught law-related courses at both the graduate and undergraduate levels for twenty-eight years. In addition to the ten novels in **The Childhood Legends Series**®, he has authored or co-authored twenty-seven adult novels and eight books of nonfiction including his recently released handbook entitled **Testifying in Court—A Guide for Peace Officers**.